Justice at Guantánamo

One Woman's Odyssey and Her Crusade for Human Rights

Kristine A. Huskey
with Aleigh Acerni

THE LYONS PRESS
Guilford, Connecticut

An imprint of The Globe Pequot Press

to my *old* family: my parents, pete and jo, my sister, kim, and grandma annie, for their unwavering support and encouragement over my lifetime, and gary maurer; to my *new* family: the di lellas, for their love; and to my husband, bryan di lella, for everything.

The Lyons Press is an imprint of The Globe Pequot Press.

Pages 51-52:
    "For strong women", from THE MOON IS ALWAYS FEMALE by Marge Piercy, copyright © 1980 by Marge Piercy. Used by permission of Alfred A. Knopf, a division of Random House, Inc.
    "For strong women" from CIRCLES ON THE WATER by Marge Piercy. Copyright © 1977, 1982 by Marge Piercy and Middlemarsh Inc. Used by permission of Wallace Literary Agency, Inc.

Cover design: Georgiana Goodwin
Cover photo: Anant Raut
Text design: Sheryl P. Kober

Library of Congress Cataloging-in-Publication Data is available on file.

ISBN 978-1-59921-468-9

Printed in the United States of America

10 9 8 7 6 5 4 3 2 1

CONTENTS

ACKNOWLEDGMENTS

I WOULD LIKE TO THANK, FIRST AND FOREMOST, ALEIGH ACERNI, for helping me tell the story of my journey through life (thus far) in a way I hope is interesting, thought-provoking, and perhaps inspiring. Aleigh spent countless hours not only listening to me talk in run-on sentences and disconnected thoughts, but also wading through some very intense memories with me; with her help, I was able to articulate much of what I was feeling. I would also like to thank Kaleena Cote, a former editor at The Globe Pequot Press, who "discovered" me and believed in my story from the beginning, as well as Ellen Urban and Lara Asher for their incredible patience and assistance in turning a lot of pages into a real book. I would also like to acknowledge the many people who have advised and inspired me throughout my legal career. Unfortunately, I didn't have enough room in this book to mention all of the lawyers, legal assistants, administrative staff, professors, journalists, doctors, NGO workers, policymakers, diplomats, clients, and U.S. servicemen and -women who have helped me over the years.

In Part II of the book, I often mention the fact that women are woefully scarce in national security law, my chosen field. I do not mean to convey that I am the *only* woman in this field, as there are many women writing, speaking about, and practicing national security legal issues, specifically relating to Guantánamo; to name a few: Beth Van Schaack, Diane Amann, Leila

Sadat, Gita Guitierrez, Agnieszka Fryszman, Beth Gilson, Candace Gorman, Sylvia Royce, Sarah Havens, Becky Dick, Hina Shamsi, Maria La Hood, Deborah Pearlstein, Karen Greenberg, Suzanne Spaulding, Kate Martin, Sahar Aziz, Barbara Olshansky and Jen Daskal. But, every one of these women will tell you that they, too, are often the only female speaker on these issues in a conference room or on a panel filled with men. The world can stand to have more women in fields that are traditionally filled by men.

Lastly, I want to thank "the girls," who have supported me 110 percent in *all* of my endeavors. They are of all ages; they are single, married, and some have children; they come from various backgrounds, nationalities, political parties, religions, and professions: Alison, Amanda, Andrea, Anna, Claire, Colleen, Debbie, Elaine, Elizabeth, Isabelle, Janie, Julie, Jenny Lee, Karen, Karishma, Kate, Katie, Lara, Laura, Lisa, Lynn, Maribel, Megan, Natalia, Sandra, and Uzma. To Girl Power.

Aleigh Acerni would like to thank: the amazing Kristine Huskey, for giving me a chance to help tell her incredible story; my mentor, Kelly Love Johnson, for being an endless source of inspiration and guidance; my parents, Mark and Jeanne Acerni, for fostering my independence and creativity; my baby sister, Vicky Acerni, for always believing that her big sister could do anything (and always being available to remind me of that); and my husband, Ian Coyne, for being, without fail, my strongest source of support for the past six years.

INTRODUCTION

"You there!" The harried-looking man pointed at me. "How much do you weigh?"

I hesitated. I still hadn't gotten used to being asked for my weight by a random stranger (who would?), although it wasn't something entirely new to me. The difference was that years ago, I was giving my measurements (along with my head shot and a whole host of other vital statistics printed on a five-by-seven card) to a casting director. Now I was being asked for my weight by a no-nonsense man in a rumpled flight uniform on the tarmac of the Fort Lauderdale airport. Back then I'd given the information in hopes of landing my next modeling photo shoot. Now I was about to board a teeny prop plane that would land at a supermax military prison on the island of Cuba.

Destination: Guantánamo.

After a fleeting urge to fib about my weight by shaving off a few pounds (a former model's first instinct), I answered the question truthfully. I'd already proffered the bundle of military passes and special security documents that proved I had permission to be on the U.S. military base. Giving a somewhat accurate weight was important; our little ten-seater plane had to be balanced. God forbid that my vanity would end up causing an improperly balanced plane to crash!

My fellow travelers and I lined up in the order directed and filed up the short stairs toward our seats. As I grasped my earplugs, I hoped that none of us would have to pee for the next three hours and forty-five minutes, since using the bathroom was a process that included a foldable screen and a chamber pot. To avoid even the slightest need to go, I had abstained from any liquids upon arriving at the airport three hours earlier. But as I sat, legs crossed, I couldn't help but think of the clients I was about to visit, who had to "do their business" without any privacy, every single day, and had done so for the last several years that they'd spent in the custody of the United States.

This trip wasn't my first time traveling to the Guantánamo U.S. Naval Base. I'd been there eight or nine times over the past year, after more than two and a half years of trying to convince the U.S. courts that the detainees at Guantánamo had a right to habeas corpus—essentially, the right to challenge one's detention. To this day, each time I head to Terminal Four, I am struck by the irony of the airline's name: When flying to Gitmo (nicknamed for Guantánamo's military abbreviation, GTMO), home to possibly the most infamous prison camp in the entire world, I take Air Sunshine. I always wondered what my clients—some of Gitmo's "enemy combatant" detainees— would think of it. Considering the details of the treatment they receive at the hands of the U.S., I don't think they'd be amused, and I don't blame them.

Once in the air, I listened to my iPod and gazed down at the ocean, which never went out of sight during the entire flight because our little plane was too small to fly above the clouds. Thankfully, I managed to avoid using the chamber pot and privacy screen; not surprisingly, every single passenger refused a drink of soda or water offered by the copilot, who also served as a flight attendant.

Despite having grown up flying on the same kind of small, loud planes during my Alaskan childhood, my confidence in them remains low. It's definitely not boosted by the fact that planes flying to Guantánamo must give Cuba a wide berth, since American planes are not allowed into Cuban airspace. This turns what should be a quick, ninety-mile flight from Miami into a nearly four-hour flight from Fort Lauderdale on a tiny turbo-prop plane. I sigh heavily on each flight when the base comes into focus; an island of browns and faded greens. And metal.

The Gitmo "airport" is mostly just a big airplane hangar. The military base at Guantánamo straddles a river that empties into a bay on the southeastern tip of the island. One side of the bay, Leeward Side, hosts the airport and lodging for the lawyers representing detainees, including Tom Wilner and Neil Koslowe, my traveling companions and colleagues from Shearman & Sterling. The bay's Windward Side is home to the majority of the base, where we're not allowed to go without a military escort, along with a McDonald's, a small Pizza Hut, a Wal-Mart-like superstore called the Naval Exchange (NEX), the "chow hall" (the cafeteria that serves free food to service members), and a couple of generic restaurants run by government contractors that serve Applebee's-style food.

When you land at Guantánamo, you show your passport to the gun-toting soldiers who greet your plane, and then hand over your security documents—a "theater clearance" and an "area clearance"—to prove you have authorization to be on the base, and, specifically, to enter the area that houses the detention center. Once those have been scrutinized and accepted, passengers get in line to have their luggage searched. The soldiers look for anything suspicious, or for items that aren't allowed on the base—although conveniently for them (and inconveniently for you), there's no written list of forbidden items, so you're not really sure what they are looking for (and honestly, I don't think they are, either).

Once we landed, I stood by, watching and wondering if any of my personal belongings would be suspect. As required, I turned on my laptop computer, and then turned it off again once it booted up. I'm not really sure what the soldiers ascertain by that exercise, but I learned on my first few trips to Gitmo that it's better not to ask. If you have a digital camera, soldiers will ask you to show them the last few pictures on it, and if you have taken any pictures of the island from the plane, they will be deleted. The principle underlying the entire Guantánamo operation (at least from a civilian point of view) is that you have no knowledge of any rules until you're on the verge of violating them. And those rules can change at any given moment.

The soldiers rifled through my stuff, pulling out bras, underwear, and other girly items. I snuck a glance at Tom, who smiled like an idiot at the free peep show. Suddenly another soldier lifted out a plastic bag and immediately turned toward me. My heartbeat quickened.

"What's this?" he asked menacingly, holding up the contents.

"Those are my vitamins," I said. And then, as if I needed some justification to have the offending vitamins in my possession, I stuttered, "I'm an athlete; a runner. I take them to stay healthy."

They really *were* vitamins, but I felt as guilty as if I'd been caught with five pounds of heroin. Being on a military base, representing "the enemy" while surrounded by U.S. soldiers, made me feel anxious about everything I did or said under their watchful eyes. Somehow, just being at Guantánamo made me feel like a prisoner myself. The soldier grunted and went back to his job. My heartbeat eventually slowed down to a normal pace while I waited for them to finish up.

After all of our bags were searched, we climbed into a white bus, which offered no air-conditioning in the hundred-degree heat, and only slight relief by way of a breeze from half of the windows that were stuck in the "down" position. We were dropped off at the CBQ (Combined Bachelor Quarters), where a mix of civilians and some visiting low-ranking military folk stay at Guantánamo. The Filipinos who had been contracted by the government to run the CBQ greeted us enthusiastically; they remembered that I am half-Filipino and that we always tip them well, giving them a twenty or so and leaving them candy and other food items that we buy here but don't consume during our stay.

On this trip, I was particularly nervous. The last time I'd been at Guantánamo, six or eight weeks earlier, I'd met with

Abdullah, one of my favorite clients. Our conversation had not gone well.

"How are you?" I'd asked. It's an awkward question to ask a detainee at Guantánamo Bay, but it was necessary.

"Not well," Abdullah said, tossing hot sauce on a vegetarian pie from Pizza Hut we'd brought for him. "I want to give you something."

"Don't you want to hear how things are going?" I asked, immediately concerned. I could tell by his tone that he really wasn't okay. Abdullah always tried to keep a positive outlook about his situation, despite the constant setbacks. On that day, however, his mood was far from positive.

"No," he answered. "Only if you have news about my family." Abdullah had four children, the youngest of which had been born after he'd been taken into custody by the U.S. He'd been at Guantánamo for over four years already. His baby daughter was growing into a little girl, and he was missing all of her important milestones.

My memory flashed to the day the Supreme Court decision came out—when the nine justices decided our clients had a right to challenge their detention in U.S. courts. I knew the decision meant I would get to visit my clients, but on that day, it was difficult to envision the reality and magnitude of sitting opposite an alleged "enemy combatant" whose waist and feet were chained to the floor in a cell at Guantánamo. And certainly, when Tom first called me into his office just six months after 9/11 to ask what I thought about the potential case, I would *never* have expected that our conversation would lead to me visiting the most infamous prison in the world. Not even in law school, filled with energy and idealistic notions of serving the public interest, had I imagined I would ever know what it felt like to be part of a case that would be heralded as the most significant civil rights case in the last twenty or thirty years.

There I was, facing Abdullah—a man who had once been on Kuwait's national soccer team, who had traveled across Europe, a somewhat-Westernized Muslim—who had been accused of being a terrorist because he'd traveled to Afghanistan wearing a watch that was common among Arab men (including some terrorists), with ten thousand dollars in cash that he planned to donate to a charitable organization. Abdullah was about twenty-eight or thirty then, and a really nice guy from what I could tell. But it was impossible to ignore his changed demeanor on that last visit. He looked defeated, exhausted. I could tell he was giving up.

"I want to give you something," he repeated. "I want you to read this to my family." He handed me a letter he had written to his loved ones, what appeared to be his last will and testament. I was shocked. I'd heard about threats of suicide from other clients before, but I'd never expected it from Abdullah, who had a lot of hope that things would work out—that he'd get the chance to prove his innocence and be released back to his family in Kuwait.

I read the letter slowly, my mind racing as I tried to figure out what to say to him. Could I be both his lawyer and his friend? His savior?

"Give me a chance, Abdullah," I pleaded, although I took his letter for safekeeping just in case. "Just wait a few more months. I think things are finally going to turn in your favor."

I wasn't simply stalling: The Kuwaiti ambassador had recently told us that a few more Kuwaitis would be released back into the custody of Kuwait. I was sure Abdullah would be one of them, but I was afraid to be that explicit. I needed to buy more time without giving him false hope. I knew he wouldn't give me a second chance if I was too specific about a release that never panned out. We talked a little longer about his wife and family, and his soccer-playing days, and finally, Abdullah agreed. He would wait to see if the diplomatic negotiations would result in his release. Neither of us spoke aloud the words that seemed to hang in the air, that if Abdullah wasn't released soon he might try to take his own life. But then, I couldn't really be sure. Maybe he gave me his will because he was sure he'd never leave Guantanamo, which was about the same as being dead to the outside world.

I had wondered then what the situation would be like in a few more months. When I returned, would Abdullah have been released as promised, or would he still be at Guantánamo? Would he still be alive? Would the government even tell me if he was dead? I doubted it; they hadn't told us when our clients had gone on a hunger strike. As far as I knew, Abdullah was still in Guantánamo, and he was still alive. But I wouldn't know for sure until I went to Camp Echo and saw him with my own eyes.

I'd never before been in the position where I felt like my own government could have such control over me, but at Gitmo, the U.S. government is the sole authority, backed up by the police and the military. At Gitmo, there is not a whole lot you can do about anything, no matter what a court back in Washington, D.C., may think you or your clients are entitled to. At Gitmo, every part of life—mine, and my clients'—was subject to military authority.

The only time I'd ever felt similarly was during the time I'd spent in Angola, feeling fairly helpless with my own persona non grata status. The civil war there had put me at risk of being picked up at any time and labeled an "enemy combatant." In fact, as an American citizen, I *was* the enemy. I was in no way a terrorist, but I recognized that even though I was perfectly innocent—as Abdullah said that he was—I still could've been picked up in a war-torn Third World country and detained by mistake.

How did I get from there to here? How am I going to make sure this guy gets the release he deserves? I knew it would take all of my strength, all of my perseverance, and every single lesson I'd learned throughout my life to come up with the right answer.

Part I: Life Then

1
Into Africa

"ANGOLA?" I PAUSED FOR A FEW MOMENTS AND THEN REPEATED the word again, this time as a statement. *Angola*. I knew, generally speaking, that Angola was in Africa, but I didn't know much else about the place. I didn't even know it was a country. I mean, I had been to Africa as a teenager, but that had been to Egypt. That's not the *real* Africa. Angola is near South Africa on the southwest coast of the continent, bordering what was formerly Zaire. I never thought I'd go to *that* part of Africa: sub-Saharan Africa of movie and literary fame; Gordimer's Africa; Heart-of-Darkness Africa; the Africa of apartheid infamy; and all that is mystical and strange but-in-a-good-way Africa. I had certainly never thought about Angola . . .

Until now, at least. My boyfriend of six months, a restaurant manager, had gotten a post with UNICEF, the United Nations International Children's Emergency Fund, which provides humanitarian aid to children all over the world who are affected by poverty and armed conflict. He was moving to Africa. Specifically, Angola.

"Do you want to go to Africa with me?" Ognjen asked, not-so-jokingly. I was eighteen. He was thirty-eight and practically right off the boat from Yugoslavia, with a mysterious Slavic accent that seemed sexy back in the eighties. We'd met at Ognjen's friend's restaurant on the Upper West Side, where I waited tables and Ognjen was the manager while he waited for his UNICEF post to come through. We'd only been dating for a few months, but growing up in the wilderness of Alaska and traveling around Europe as a teen had given me an adventurous spirit, and he knew it. Angola sounded interesting and a little dangerous—an exciting change from my "exhilarating" life as a dancer-turned-waitress who'd moved to New York City to make her dreams come true. (As if no girl's ever done that before.)

I cringed as I thought of the tiny, two-bedroom, dungeon-like basement apartment I shared with three other women. It was *technically* in Manhattan, but so close to the Bronx that one could almost hear the crack of the bat at Yankee Stadium. Moving to New York was supposed to make me famous—at least a little bit—but five months after moving to the Big Apple, I had quit taking dance classes, preferring to dance on bars and at clubs when I wasn't waitressing. My focus had drifted to making sure the rent was paid each month instead of perfecting my turnout and arabesque.

And then there was the break-in. A few weeks earlier, the apartment I shared with my sister, Kim, and two other girls I'd gone to high school with had been completely vandalized and burglarized. We'd come home to find lipstick graffiti on the walls and mirrors emblazoned with DIE WHITE BITCHES. Every piece of furniture was overturned, photos were rifled through, and anything of value had been stolen. It was an invasion of privacy. It was intimidating. The graffiti made it unmistakably clear that the break-in was not random; we were, in fact, the only white girls in a predominantly Dominican neighborhood. Around the same time, we received a pretty serious dose of New York City's resident virus—otherwise known as a cockroach and rat infestation.

"I'll go," I finally said. "Show me where Angola is on a map."

A month later, after Ognjen had gotten settled in Angola, I had myself vaccinated against typhoid and yellow fever and all the other nasty African plagues you can imagine. I refused, however, to take any malaria pills; I wasn't sure how long I was going to be there, and I'd heard that there were fairly severe side effects. Besides, no doctor would give me a malaria prescription for "time period: indefinite." Reading the list of health warnings about traveling in Angola was pretty frightening:

Don't drink the water or use ice.

Don't swim in fresh water.

Don't eat dairy products.

Keep your hands and feet dry to prevent parasitic infections.

Avoid mosquitoes, snakes, flies, animals, needles, nighttime, crowded places.

Avoid flies and crowded places? I was going to a capital city in Africa, for bloody goodness' sake! Despite the warnings, though, I was ready—and excited. Spending my high school years at a boarding school thousands of miles from where my parents lived (we'd moved to Saudi Arabia from my childhood home in Alaska for my father to work as a pilot for ARAMCO, an oil company, but I'd had to return to the U.S. to attend high school), I'd developed a healthy sense of independence. Living self-sufficiently in New York City had only strengthened my autonomy. It felt good, and strangely powerful.

My parents, by the way, didn't have much of a say in my decision. What could they say? I was an adult. I'd been living on my own in New York City with no obligations, monetary or otherwise, to them. They weren't supporting me while I played out my I'm-going-to-New-York-to-be-a-dancer dream. I was very close with my parents, growing up—Kim and I both were. They had taken us everywhere; we did everything as a family. In the winter, we went to all of my father's amateur hockey games; in summer, we loaded up the family floatplane every weekend to go fishing and hunting in the remote Alaska wilderness; and both of my parents came to every dance recital Kim and I danced in. But when you go away to boarding school at fourteen and your parents live thousands of miles away, and your relationship becomes a phone call once a week, you start to depend on yourself pretty quickly. It's not that we weren't still close; it was that the physical distance made me much more independent; that, and paying my own rent and everything else at the age of seventeen.

I scribbled down my relocation plans to them in a brief

letter, which I asked Kim to graciously read to them over the phone the next time they called from Saudi Arabia. To this day, I continue to have a bit of nagging guilt—both from making my sister the bearer of this kind of news, and from letting my parents know of my move in such an impersonal and crude way:

Dear Mom and Dad:

I'm going to Africa . . . specifically, Angola.

Good-bye!

2

Surviving a Civil War

I WAS FILLED WITH AN INTENSE NERVOUS ENERGY AS I BOARDED the plane for Angola. I'd spent very little time researching my new home (there was no Internet back then; imagine going to the library to do research—the horror!), but I did know that the fall of 1985 was definitely not a great time to be headed there. The country was embroiled in a heated civil war that had begun in the 1970s when the Portuguese, the colonial rulers, were finally kicked out by local entities vying for power. Ognjen had been sent to Africa, to a country whose current Marxist government was being supported monetarily and with expertise by what was then the Union of Soviet Socialist Republics (USSR). The rebel group, National Union for the Total Independence of Angola (UNITA)—or "insurgents," as we would call them today—was led by Jonas Savimbi and funded by another world superpower: the United States of America, my home and place of citizenship.

Although I was living in the midst of a civil war that would last for twenty-seven years, during which more than five hundred thousand people would die, my first few months in Angola weren't very exciting—or even particularly dangerous. As a young woman living in the capital city of Luanda without diplomatic status, I was already persona non grata. As an American citizen, however, I was sometimes seen as "the enemy" by people I'd meet casually at social events. Often, our conversations didn't get very far: "Nice night, eh? How's your martini? Uh-huh. You're American? Oh."

In those first few months, my greatest fear was not getting blown up or contracting malaria but rather getting snubbed by some Euro-diplomat who already disliked America for its lack of national health care. Some people, however, thought I was a spy for the CIA simply because of my nationality, which I think was one reason I found myself a frequent guest in the home of the wife of the First Secretary of the Soviet Embassy, who was constantly confiding in me.

"They think you're CIA," Ognjen would joke. "Forget your age. She tells you something, you tell her something."

Technically I *was* a citizen of the enemy, but I suppose being eighteen years old (and looking it) prevented me from being seriously suspected. I'm sure things would be different today, having seen how the United States has treated Omar Khadr, my former "enemy-combatant" client and alleged "child al-Qaeda," at Guantánamo Bay. But I'm getting ahead of myself.

I didn't have an Angolan work visa and I wasn't posted with any embassy. Because I wasn't married to Ognjen, I didn't have United Nations (UN) status, either, which would have at least provided diplomatic protection of some kind had I ever been picked up by a soldier, either informally—meaning arbitrarily and lawlessly (which almost happened once)—or formally, meaning arrested, or had we ever had to evacuate the city (which was not unlikely given the proximity of the fighting). UN status would have also made traveling alone easier, both inside and outside the city, allowing me the freedom to explore with some level of comfort.

Ognjen and I first lived in an apartment building in the middle of what had once been a beautiful city, but by the mid- to late-1980s, the city of Luanda was a nightmare—beyond the usual Third World big-city chaos. The city had seen fighting for over fifteen years by the time I arrived, and it showed. There simply was no infrastructure: no trash collection, no postal system, no serious mass transportation system, hardly any buses running (those that did were packed, with people literally hanging out of the doors), and few working streetlights (including the traffic lights). Vehicles that had been left behind when the Portuguese fled had been appropriated by the few Angolans who could figure out how to start them and keep them running; many cars just littered the roadsides or were turned into shelters by refugees. Our neighborhood was certainly not the kind of place where you could go for a casual stroll; in fact, there weren't many places in the city where a young female Westerner would be welcome.

There was a decent-sized community of Westerners in Luanda, which was further divided into two groups: the "do-gooders," which consisted of diplomats (those who worked for the UN or an embassy) and relief workers (people working for some humanitarian organization), and then the business-people, most of whom worked for oil companies, as northern

Angola was rich in oil. There were also a number of workers from the Third World, and a larger, albeit aloof, community of Brazilians. And then there were the "locals"—the Angolans (both those viewed as truly native to Africa, and those who had been mixing with the Portuguese for the last five hundred years but still considered themselves native Angolans), and a lot of refugees, displaced due to the war in Angola or some other African conflict, streaming in and out of Luanda and surrounding environs.

The refugees and many of the locals looked just as you might imagine: kids with very little clothing, no shoes, big bellies, and looks of disbelief; women wearing colorful dresses with gigantic tubs of laundry or sacks of rice balanced on their heads; men without shirts, revealing scars that come from a little native insect that lays its eggs in damp clothing; once hatched, the flies burrow into the skin to hatch later on. There were kids and adults with missing limbs, blown off by mines left behind or as a result of direct fighting.

Unless you had a special pass, which was granted by the government and usually provided to top embassy diplomats and very high-ranking UN officials, you were not allowed to be outdoors past the midnight curfew, and you weren't allowed to travel more than fifty kilometers (about thirty miles) outside of the city without permission, which I never could have gotten with my persona non grata status anyway. There were very few roads that cars could travel on, making it relatively easy for the military to track movement in and out of the city with just a few scant checkpoints scattered along Luanda's perimeter.

On a few occasions, Ognjen and I violated the curfew, driving through a deserted Luanda after midnight on our way home from a UN or embassy function. I used to wonder, had we been stopped by soldiers, would it have been better to show my U.S. passport or to be without any identification at all? (Would there have been more or less reason to arrest me in either case?) Thankfully, I never had to find out.

All of this came down to one thing: I was stuck. Stuck in a small apartment without air-conditioning during the ninety-degree heat of the day, and stuck in the apartment at night. I did a lot of reading and snacking, putting on at least ten pounds (there's no greater sin for a former ballet dancer). Occasionally I would be released from captivity when we would have dinner with some of Ognjen's friends from the Yugoslavian embassy. Since my boyfriend was from Yugoslavia (before the country broke up into little pieces that then engaged in their own civil wars), his native language was Serbo-Croatian. Many of Ognjen's "Yugo" friends spoke very little English, so they would speak in their native tongue most of the time, even when I was around. As a result, I picked up some Serbo-Croatian, learning a number of great swear words, the nastiest of which sounds like "Machu Picchu" (the awe-inspiring religious Inca structure in Peru).

We got a puppy to keep me company, a little Rottweiler named Shaba, named for the area in Kenya that Joy Adamson of *Born Free* fame used as the setting for several books, including *Queen of Shaba*. I spent much of the first six months of my time in Angola training her. Shaba grew up not to be the great guard dog for my protection that we'd originally hoped for, but a rather friendly beast that was often very timid. I take full credit for this anomaly.

Eventually Ognjen and I moved to a different area of the city, where a large population of Portuguese nationals had lived when Angola existed as a Portuguese colony. It was a nice, suburban-like residential area, a gated community of sorts. Indeed, almost every house in our new neighborhood had typical Third World, sturdy metal-sheeted fencing with locked gates. From the streets you could see the luscious tropical trees standing tall, spreading their canopies over the red-tiled rooftops, and the brightly colored flowers creeping over the edges of the metal walls.

Here, I could take Shaba for walks around the neighborhood and go jogging. On these jaunts, I'd see three types of people entering and leaving the houses: the white Westerners; the affluent, lighter-colored natives (a common vestige of European domination in the Third World); and the dark Angolan servants. In hindsight, it was all very African and disturbingly reminiscent of colonialism—the dark-skinned underclass serving the light-skinned (both white and mixed) elite, but at the time, it was simply the reality in which I was living. Ognjen and I had three servants ourselves: a gruff young woman who came to clean (mind you, I did not begrudge her her surliness, as I was well aware of the painful dynamics in our relationship); a smiling young man who worked in our garden; and an older woman who was infinitely patient with me, a naïve young white girl whose clothing cost more than her yearly salary. With only the kindest of looks, Maria taught me how to negotiate the complexities of living in such circumstances.

Civil war meant that even though we now had a house with everyday commodities like air-conditioning and running water—luxuries compared to what the local population had—the city's crumbling infrastructure couldn't always sustain them. We would often go for days at a time without running water, and at least twice a week we would be without electricity. On several occasions, we had no electricity for the entire week. We did not have a television or many appliances that would have required electricity, but that was the least of our problems. It was a daily struggle simply to figure out how to make dinner or wash dishes without the necessary ingredients (running water) or facilities (electricity).

I learned to take extremely short showers to conserve the water in our tank, and to take "splash baths" from a jerry can filled with water we'd surreptitiously siphoned from the side of the UN building. I learned not to drink the tap water, to soak vegetables in a special cleaning solution before cooking them, to iron every piece of clothing for fear of the fly that had left its physical mark on so many natives and refugees. We had no phone, no radio, no hair or clothing dryer; we had bread shortages all the time, and my attempts at making bread were quite short-lived after I twice tried to serve Ognjen homemade bread with the density of a cement block. Some things I just never saw the entire time I was there—certain vegetables, like broccoli and mushrooms, and pharmacy items, like cotton balls. And we were the Westerners—living as diplomats to boot—who still had so much *more* than most of the population. It was here in Angola that I also learned there are very few things a person truly needs to live.

Maria taught me how to shop for the basics. We would go to the local open-air market in the outskirts of the city, me as the driver, Maria as the guide. It was big, loud, and bustling with positive energy despite the circumstances. The farmers, usually women, had their wares laid out on burlaps sacks on the ground—vegetables that were very sad and limp, but I bought some, nonetheless. I also bought oil here, and anything else that looked edible to my Western eyes, instead of from the government-run grocery store, which had very little to offer in the way of produce.

The market was frequented by both locals and Westerners in oddly equal amounts. There was an outrageous black market in currency exchange at the time. On the black market, one U.S. dollar was worth 1,200 to 1,500 kwanzas, sometimes more, depending on how the war was going. The *official* exchange rate, however, was one U.S. dollar to thirty kwanzas. This meant that for Angolans working for the government and getting paid in kwanzas, the price of a few tomatoes in the farmers' market was fifty times as much as in the government store, which was, more often than not, completely devoid of fresh produce anyway. Why would a local farmer sell her wares to the government when she could get a much better price in the market? None of this really affected me, however, as Ognjen was paid in dollars, and exchanging dollars at the black market exchange rate was fairly easy. I wondered about a Marxist system that in theory brings social and economic equality to all, yet in reality, as far as I could see, brought nothing but inequities—at least in wartime.

I was painfully aware of my position of privilege, and while it disturbed me, it also forced me to question global relations and economy, different social policies, and the like— all at an age when most of my peers were wondering whether Mom and Dad would buy them a new or a used car. Despite my deep misgivings, however, I did not eschew the benefits. I was busy learning to survive in other ways, myself, as very few people spoke English in Angola, even the diplomats. It was, after all, a Portuguese-speaking country. When I first arrived, I often had to rely on my rusty high school French, but eventually I did manage to pick up enough Portuguese to communicate, and six months into my stay, I was speaking it fluently. I also taught English to a few adults—an Angolan man and a couple of Brazilian women—mainly to keep myself occupied. In fact, my Angolan student worked for the government, and if he'd paid me at the government exchange rate, it would have been equivalent to nickels and dimes on the market. He insisted on paying me something—a set of sheets, a can of oil, a sack of sugar—important commodities in a civil war.

I also soon began to understand what it really meant to live in a country that is in the middle of an armed conflict, apart from the lack of everyday conveniences and bountiful produce. One day, driving along by myself in a little white Renault 4 we'd had shipped from France, I pulled up to a stoplight. On the sidewalk, about fifteen feet away, stood a small group of Angolan soldiers sporting military fatigues and machine guns. There were always soldiers on the streets, in the airport, everywhere; in fact, there were over twenty-two thousand Soviet and Cuban soldiers in Luanda alone, not to mention the Angolan army—and they were all carrying machine guns. Suddenly, one of them started to walk toward the passenger side of my car. He was weaving a little, and looked drunk. I hurriedly leaned over and pushed the lock down (automatic locks were not ubiquitous back then, and my car was a standard, basic and cheap).

"Oh God!" I said aloud to myself (even as my strong Catholic upbringing had me whispering, "Mom, please forgive me for taking the Lord's name in vain").

The soldier tried the passenger-side door, leering at me through the window, and then began walking toward the back of the car. *Holy shit!* I thought (that one was maybe not so forgivable). I locked the driver-side door and sped straight through the red light, admittedly peeing my pants a little, and madly wondering if I was carrying my passport or whether I should pretend that I didn't have any identification at all. I have no idea what would have happened to me that day if he'd succeeded in getting into my car. Most Western women never went out alone; they always took a servant or a friend with them when they went out, even during the day. I never heard of any Western women getting hurt or being kidnapped, but I was certainly relieved not to be the first.

After that experience, I realized how much everything around me was intimately affected by the war. The natives were clearly suffering from starvation, disease, land mines, the direct fighting, and displacement. There were a number of foreigners (mostly from Western countries) who were living in the city and traveling the countryside, often without government permission, trying to provide humanitarian aid to Angolans and other refugees. There were enough Westerners in Luanda that most of the time no one stared at me or seemed to think I looked out of place, even though there weren't any tourists. If you were white, it was assumed you were working for a relief organization or an embassy. There were also a number of foreigners who were there for legitimate business purposes (mostly related to the oil wells in the north), and some who were trying to exploit the situation. They, too, traveled around the city and the countryside, despite the fighting and movement of troops.

On the one hand, it was all chaos begat by war, but on the other hand, everyone was just trying to live some kind of a normal life, whatever that meant. We got dressed up and went to UN and embassy functions, and we put on our swimwear and went to the beach in groups, with coolers full of whiskey and sandwiches, all while a civil war raged on in the background. We traveled outside the country to Italy, Yugoslavia, and even back to the States twice—once to visit my sister in New York, and once to visit my parents, who had moved back to Alaska from Saudi Arabia. But we always returned to Angola and the ongoing war, so Ognjen could get back to his job as chief officer of the UNICEF Emergency Project (which sounded pretty vague and all-encompassing considering the circumstances). I couldn't get my mind around the contradictions that surrounded me. The war and all its soldiers and guns and fighting existed alongside the plethora of civilians—the aid workers, the businessmen, and the local population—trying to feed their kids, do some good, or make enough money just to get by.

Shortly after the incident with the soldier, I had another frightening ordeal—this time with my health. I had gotten my period as usual, but after two weeks, it hadn't stopped. I was still bleeding, and heavily. I knew I needed to see a doctor, but who could I see? There were both communication *and* trust issues. How could I trust a doctor I couldn't even understand?

Eventually, I was directed to a UNICEF colleague of Ognjen's who worked in an Angolan hospital. It was terrifying: There were two or three people together in one hospital bed (yes, one *bed*, not one room); it was filthy with dirt and flies. After a few questions and a cursory examination, the colleague simply said, "You must go see a doctor, but not here. This hospital is not for you."

Apparently there were different services for the locals and the expats. I didn't need to be told twice to go elsewhere, but the fact that I was a person without status and there was no organization responsible for me or my health made things a bit more complicated. I didn't know where to go. Finally, realizing the former Soviet Union had a health clinic of its own, the wife of one of the Yugos and I decided to try to beg our way in.

"Please," Deuschtsza pleaded, speaking a mixture of Serbo-Croatian and another language I couldn't understand. "This young girl is bleeding and we have nowhere else to go."

I was scared. My thoughts were deafening—*please have pity on me, please have pity on me*—but I knew that it was important for me to keep absolutely silent. I didn't want the Soviets to know that I was American or that I spoke English, for fear they would think, as others had, that I was a spy for the United States. This time it really mattered. It was the height of irony: An American girl, whose native country has wonderful, modern health-care services for people with some money, begging for basic health care from the Soviets during the Cold War.

Finally the clinic agreed to see me, and a woman examined me. I have no idea what kind of doctor she was—or even if she was a doctor—and the entire process unfolded via a not-so-great translation. I was given two shots—one through an IV in my arm, the other a shot in my butt. I still don't know what the shots were or what, exactly, they were for, and no one could explain it to me. The woman treated me and let me go, with barely a word. A few days later I stopped bleeding. These are the things you don't think of when your boyfriend asks you to move to Angola with him and, on a whim, you say yes.

I spent almost two years living in Angola before I decided it was time to move on. I had come to the country as an eighteen-year-old girl with no college education in order to escape my previous life and to have a glorious adventure in Africa, and I left as a twenty-year-old woman with a desire to find a passion that would define me. I was ready to return to New York.

"Of course I love you," I said to Ognjen when I told him I had to leave. Truthfully, though, I wasn't so sure. I cared about him, without a doubt, but I had moved to Angola just six months into our relationship. We had depended on each other and formed a bond through stress and necessity, but I found that my longing to return to civilization was stronger than my desire to stay in Angola with Ognjen.

"I need more. I can't get a job here," I explained. "I can't get an education. I have to move on." Ognjen understood, but he couldn't leave; he was destined for this kind of life. When he tracked me down in Washington, D.C., years later, I learned that after Angola, he stayed with UNICEF, moving on to more war-torn countries—first Afghanistan, and then Cambodia. The last time we spoke, a few years ago, he was in Switzerland awaiting a new post.

I was sad to leave Ognjen and Shaba and the life we had been living, but as my plane lifted off the runway, I had to suppress the urge to giggle. It was the most incredible feeling of relief and freedom—my heart felt lighter and lighter the higher we soared.

3

A Year of Living Dangerously

By THE TIME MY PLANE LANDED IN NEW YORK, I WAS FULLY ready to embrace what Angola had not been able to offer: jobs, restaurants, retail shopping, mass transportation, people my age and with whom I shared a common language and similar circumstances. The future looked bright and full of opportunity.

It never occurred to me that in returning to the U.S., life might actually seem a bit ho-hum (even in New York) after the daily worries and adrenaline rush that had been my life in Angola. My homecoming was entirely without the kind of fanfare you might expect for a girl returning from a somewhat perilous life in a place like Angola. As nonchalantly as if I'd been getting off the shuttle from Washington, D.C.—instead of flying in from the Third World—I simply got off the plane, collected my luggage, and took a taxi, alone, from the airport to my sister's apartment in Manhattan. I hadn't been expecting flowers and champagne (although champagne would have been nice), but I also hadn't really told anyone I was moving back to the States, either. I had briefly mentioned to Kim during one of our rare phone calls that I'd eventually come home, but I never told her that I was getting on a plane on a specific date.

Direct and instantaneous communication from Angola was rare. Cell phones and the Internet weren't an option in 1987, and because we didn't have our own house phone in Luanda, calling from Angola involved a series of difficult maneuvers, and we didn't always get through to the States. My sister had made sure I still had a key to her apartment, but still, when I lumbered up the four little stairs from the foyer into her apartment at 30 Gold Street, down by the South Street Seaport, dragging my luggage, she was shocked.

"Oh!" she said. Then, playing it cool: "Hello, Krissy."

"Hi," I said, travel-weary but matter-of-fact. "I decided to move back to New York."

We were all frozen in place, waiting for someone else to make the first move. Kim hadn't budged; her roommate, Rhonda, a girl with whom we'd gone to high school, and whom we'd affectionately dubbed "Rhoda Red" for her fiery red hair, was poised on the edge of a chair, watching the scene unfold. "Hi, Krissy!" she said in her endlessly cheery Midwestern way. We all hugged; I was home.

I didn't have to ask if I could stay; I knew Kim wouldn't mind. Though she was only ten and a half months older than me, during those early days back in New York, she really was "the older sister," always looking out for me. She was a great, stable force in my life, and I knew that moving into the one-bedroom apartment she and Rhonda shared wouldn't be a problem.

I was delighted to be in a place with running water, a television, and access to fresh broccoli at the grocery store. Although I'd realized while living in Angola that I could get by without having much, I was certainly grateful for long, hot showers and friends who spoke English. It did take a little while to get readjusted to life in New York, however; I was always turning the water off quickly (a habit I'd developed in Angola to help conserve the water in our tank), until our good friend Bridget Knapp, one of the original toddlers in the famous Coppertone ad in the 1960s jokingly said to me, "In *America*, we can run the water *while* we do the dishes." (Nobody was worried about being "green" back then.)

I would often muse aloud about how thankful I was to be able to buy an apple and not have to worry about whether it would give me a bacterial infection. I was also thrilled that I didn't have to iron every single item of clothing, since I'd left that nasty burrowing fly behind in Angola. Eventually, though, I was spending less time being thankful for public transportation, working streetlights, and robust vegetables; needing a job that helped to pay the rent became my sole focus. Kim helped me find a job waitressing at a busy restaurant in the Village.

Bar Lui was a somewhat well-known Italian bar and restaurant on Broadway, between Houston and Bleecker. It ran the length of an entire city block and had infamous lights on the walls—infamous because they looked a little bit like breasts with nipples, just enough to be slightly titillating without being crass. Despite its trendiness, the food was fairly good, as were the Italian wines. It was so popular that on Friday and Saturday nights we had ultra-eighties red velvet ropes and bouncers outside, to keep out the uncool, the not-so-hip, and the "bridge-

and-tunnel" crowd, as we used to refer to people coming in from outside Manhattan for the weekend. We usually had a pretty steady crowd of trendy-looking customers on the weekends, there "to see and be seen."

One night I waited on a guy sitting by himself at a table for two. He introduced himself and asked if I'd ever thought about modeling.

"Not really," I replied, thinking, *Of course I had! What pretty girl in New York City doesn't at least toy with the idea for five seconds?* But I hadn't thought about it with any seriousness. It wasn't that I was uninterested or felt threatened by Lenny— he looked like a teddy-bear version of Mr. T with John Lennon glasses and a puka-shell necklace—but it was a busy night, and I didn't have much interest in chatting with a guy about modeling when I had a ton of hungry, drunk customers who would help pay the bills.

"How about if I take some pictures of you?" Lenny asked. He was persistent; I had to give him that. I looked at him sideways. He seemed nice enough and he really did look harmless. "For free," he added.

What the hell? I thought. *What do I have to lose?* After all, I'd originally come to New York to be a famous dancer; maybe this was an opportunity to do something a little more glamorous than fetching drinks and four-cheese ravioli.

"Sure," I agreed, handing him his bill. "Why not?"

A few days later, I met him at his studio and he took some pictures in his apartment/studio in the Village. He had those large, strong lights on tripods, and the silver umbrella-looking things to reflect the light. So, he really was a photographer! I brought jeans and some nice tops; he shot mostly from the waist up, just to try me out in front of the camera. I was lucky (my instincts about people are usually good), and he didn't try anything weird or ask me to take my clothes off (which I would've refused, but would have made for an awkward situation). It was fun posing in front of a camera, pretending to be a model, and I surprised myself by having a good time.

Maybe I have something here, I thought. Then I quickly reminded myself of how many gorgeous women live in New York with the *sole* goal of making it as a model—women who are both taller and skinnier than me, the two most prized (and sometimes seemingly the only required) features of a model. Posing for Lenny was fun, but I didn't have a plan for what to do with the photos when I had them—not yet, anyway.

I'd been working at Bar Lui for a few months when once again, I was approached about modeling. This time it was a man *and* a woman—very legit—and they asked if I'd be interested in auditioning for an MTV video, with "some" dance experience required. I didn't hesitate. "Sure," I said. "Give me the details."

The audition was in a loft in Tribeca, only it wasn't really like the ones I'd faced as a dancer at Interlochen Arts Academy, the performing arts boarding high school I'd attended. Then, we had to audition for roles in the upcoming dance concerts by *actually dancing*, usually for a solid hour or two.

In contrast, the MTV audition was over before I knew it. I hadn't put together a "book" (a portfolio of pictures), nor had I taken the time to get any of Lenny's shots enlarged. I didn't have anything to give the casting directors, which they said was not a problem. They took a Polaroid. A Polaroid! I had learned that the directors were looking for different types of ethnic women to dance in the video, which was the likely reason I had been approached in the first place. My Filipino mother's features and my Caucasian father's tall, lanky body type made for an interesting combination. I tried to help my chances by telling them how much dance training I had.

"I was a real dancer, you know," I offered.

"Move a little to your left," was the response.

"At a school for performing arts," I added. "We used to tour—and perform three or four times a year." Was I stuttering? Too eager? I couldn't help myself. I desperately wanted the job.

"Okay, smile!"

"I danced five to seven hours a day."

"You did? That's nice. Next!"

Either my "audition" impressed the casting director, or I just happened to have the kind of look they were going for, because I was hired to be a model/dancer in Buster Poindexter's "Hot, Hot, Hot" video. It was a very small part (translation: microscopic), but it was my first real taste of life as a model—getting my hair and makeup done, having a dress chosen for me, models running around half-clothed, giggling and smoking, overhearing snobby conversations from the more experienced models, and realizing how much of a newbie I was—just another girl in New York City trying to make it as a model.

Fellow model Elaine Chu took me under her wing—a complete rarity in the modeling world—and actually talked to me that day as if we were colleagues. Even after the shoot, Elaine continued to nurture me and give me advice on all things modeling. She taught me about "height inflation" and "weight deflation." This was shorthand for: When asked by anybody, including casting directors, agencies, other models, and even your local grocer, always add an inch or two to your real height and subtract several pounds from your real weight. Or, even better, don't bother weighing yourself—just make up a number.

She also confirmed that being ethnic was an advantage in the modeling world. Elaine's married name was Luke, but she used her maiden name professionally, because "Elaine Chu" was invited to any and all Asian auditions, while "Elaine Luke" was just another white girl competing with thousands of other white girls for every modeling spot. I wondered what "Huskey" conveyed. I hoped it sounded thin. And tall.

The day of the video shoot was cold and rainy. I danced in Chinatown with about ten other Asian-looking girls and a few non-Asian girls wearing Suzie Wong dresses and trying to look hot, hot, hot despite the fact that we were shivering to death in our thin dresses. The ten-second scene took several hours to shoot in order to get "the look" just right—meaning numerous attractive young women in the streets of Chinatown spontaneously dancing in circles around a singing white man sporting a tux and a pompadour hairstyle. It's a glamorous lifestyle, sure, but modeling is *hard work*. A few weeks after the shoot, Buster Poindexter, otherwise known as David Johansen of The New York Dolls, invited the models to his show at The Bitter End. We had VIP seating, and some of the band members actually came up to the table and talked to us. I felt like I had arrived.

Shortly after my music video debut, I decided that waitressing wasn't nearly as exciting or profitable as bartending. My sister had been bartending at Lucy's, a New York surfer bar, and I would go there to hang out, drink for free, and watch her work the bar. The bartender has so much control. You're in charge of the bar; you're in charge of the booze. Everyone loves the bartender—not only the customers and the bar-backs, but the managers and bouncers, the wait staff and busboys; the bartender is king (or queen, as was the case with Kim). And during the late eighties, Manhattan was *Bright Lights, Big City*; it was party central. Reaganomics was in full effect, so bankers, lawyers, and Wall Street suits had cash to burn, and the stock market hadn't crashed yet. People were partying—a lot—and being generous with their tips. When the stock market did crash in October of 1987, spending slowed down some, but people still went out for cocktails. It was the Big Apple, after all!

Bartenders at Bar Lui wore leopard-skin bras, corsets, and black miniskirts while working; they danced on the bar and did shots with customers. One slow Sunday night, Darrow, a spirited girl with hippie parents and a sister named Rainbow, won a bet with her customers by doing twenty push-ups on the bar. I knew I could do it (the bartending, not the push-ups), or at least look good trying. And apparently my managers thought so, too. I just had to learn how to mix drinks. I was given the Saturday day shift to start and quickly moved on to substituting behind the bar some evenings. Eventually I was given my own night shifts.

Working in a restaurant had already introduced me to a strange but tantalizing lifestyle. I had apprenticed as a New York–style partier while I was waitressing, but bartending promoted me to professional status. I became ensnared in the frenetic partying scene that was such a part of life in NYC. I was making good money, customers were buying me shots, and I was buying them shots and pouring myself one, too—it was basically a party that I just happened to get paid to attend every night.

After our shifts ended, Kim and I would go out and party some more, quickly discovering the after-hours establishments that were illegally serving alcohol after four a.m. Sometimes they were in run-down lofts that had a card table set up with bottles of hard liquor, club soda, Diet Coke, and plastic cups, often with no ice. Then there were some real bars that were also open after hours: The lights would be off, you'd need to know a special knock or password to get in the door, and the place would be *packed*—as if it were only midnight instead of five in the morning.

It was a time of little consequences, and I had an appetite for risk and adventure, which ultimately turned into one for self-destruction. Drugs seemed to be everywhere, especially coke. If you went to the bathroom and saw more than one pair of feet in a stall, you knew what was going on in there. I saw everyone from busboys to movie stars doing coke—either behind the scenes, or right at their tables. My friends were the people who were willing to go out with me after my bar shift ended, or who knew a bouncer at a cool club, or who were hip enough to go with me to a dance club, walk nonchalantly up to the front of a very long line, and get "chosen" by the bouncer to enter. I always got chosen—and was proud of this fact— and I didn't want to be dragged down by anybody who looked or acted like they might not get picked. I loved going to The World—a big dance club near Houston Street on the East Side, where they'd play *Pump Up the Volume* every night—because the bouncer knew me and I never had to wait in line. This was important back then.

I knew I'd hit bottom, but it wasn't when I threw up in a cab for the umpteenth time, or when I realized that I'd already had six or seven Sex on the Beach shots before ten p.m. while working behind the bar. It was when I found myself coming home one morning from a night out. Returning as the sun was rising had been occurring more and more frequently, but this time it was ten a.m. and I was dressed in a black velvet cock- tail dress I had borrowed from Kim—and I wasn't wearing any shoes. It was a beautiful sunny day and I wished for sunglasses.

Of course, why would I have sunglasses with me since I'd gone out at night? (And why was I wearing velvet after Easter?) It was a weekday, and people in dark business suits were striding intently down the sidewalk to begin their workdays. I took the subway to get home. I wasn't sure where I'd been.

Sadly, my mess of a life wasn't just about the all-night drinking and dancing; my home life was becoming a calamity, too. I'd moved into a beautiful, brand-new, two-bedroom apartment in a run-down building that was being renovated apartment by apartment, on 109th Street and Amsterdam. My new roommate was Becky, my former roommate from Interlochen, who'd moved to New York to attend Juilliard. It was time to stop relying on Kim for everything, and—bonus—I was thrilled to have my own bedroom. I'd anguished over telling my sister that I was leaving. We were so close it was like telling her we were going under the knife to separate our attached bodies.

New York was a block-by-block town when it came to livable neighborhoods. One block too far to the east, west, north, or south and it was a whole other world. Though it was less than ten blocks from Columbia University, our neighborhood was very shabby, with young men hanging out on the stoops, leering and looking intimidating.

"Yo, Mam-mie!" they'd yell over their open beers. "*Mamacita!*"

Our neighbors were mostly low-income Hispanics who were likely going to get kicked out of their homes by our landlord's gentrification efforts, and they didn't seem keen on having two young "white" girls, who were advancing this effort, as neighbors. To me, being considered a "white girl" by my Hispanic neighbors, but "ethnic-looking" by music video casting directors, was not a surprise. I'd gotten used to being asked at work how I had learned to speak English so well, or what country I was from. When I said, "America," I was met with blank stares. (Is it really that hard to believe that a girl who is half Filipino, half Caucasian, could actually have been born in this country?)

Our fabulous, newly constructed apartment was a problem from the get-go, and the management company, despite seemingly good intentions, turned out to be completely useless. Though we had signed a lease for a two-bedroom apartment, by the time the move-in date rolled around, the new apartment was still being renovated, so they put us in a one-bedroom in the same building. Okay. No problem. I was disappointed to not have my own bedroom, but I wasn't about to jeopardize our ability to move into the building by complaining. The one-bedroom was also brand-new, quite lovely, and our rent was cheaper. The fact that there was no refrigerator didn't seem to be such a big deal at first, but after a few weeks and many excuses by management, it was starting to get old.

Eventually, we moved up to our two-bedroom on the fifth floor, which had a refrigerator but no kitchen window! Now, I had seen many New York apartments the size of a shoe box that were completely windowless, or were lacking kitchens altogether; in this case, however, there was a window-shaped square cut out of the kitchen wall where the kitchen window *should* have been. The kitchen "window" looked over the narrow alley between our building and the neighboring building. Not only could you see the neighbors, but you could also reach right through the empty space and touch them as well!

Then there was the radiator, which apparently hadn't been part of the renovations; it was old, and strained so much that one crisp winter morning it groaned and chuckled and then quasi-exploded, blowing steam like a boiling teakettle. The window overlooking the fire escape at the back of the building was another problem: It had no locks, and although we'd complained several times, our fifth-floor apartment was eventually broken into. Whatever valuables that hadn't been stolen in my first New York robbery were taken in the second— although thankfully, this time there weren't threatening messages scrawled on the mirrors and walls. Instead, as if we didn't already feel vulnerable enough, we developed a stalker.

The phone suddenly rang one day as my key turned in the lock. I slammed the door, dropped my backpack, and ran to the phone.

"Hello?"

"I know you're home," a female voice said. I didn't recognize it. "You better watch out."

This became a routine. Becky and I would walk in the door and the phone would ring immediately.

"I know you just walked in the door," she said. Sometimes it would be a male voice, making similar threats. It didn't seem like a big deal until later, when the threats started happening more frequently. A few weeks later, the word *sluts* was painted on our mailbox in what looked like red nail polish. Next we found a vague but threatening note on the door. The messages and phone calls became increasingly aggressive, and Becky was starting to freak out.

"I can't stay here anymore, Krissy. My parents want me to leave." She was apologetic. "I'm going to stay with friends of my grandmother's, at least for now."

I couldn't just move and break the lease. I was stuck, again. Kim was living with her boyfriend, my parents were thousands of miles away in Alaska, and my friends in New York had limited living space. I wasn't going to ask for help, and I wasn't about to leave New York because of some crazy stalker. I was definitely nervous, however, and Becky's decision to stay elsewhere, temporarily or otherwise, made me feel more vulnerable.

I couldn't help feeling some disdain for Becky's decision. I knew it was definitely the safest thing to do, but I thought her financial dependence on her parents made her weak. Wasn't her inability to stay when the going got tough proof enough? Everyone had conflicting advice for me. "Stick it out, Kristine," my father said in his tough-as-nails Alaskan way. My dad could build a fire in an ice storm while shielding us from a bear attack, and he expected his girls to survive under any circumstances, too. "Don't let them push you around."

My sister disagreed. "Just leave, Krissy," she said. "Dad doesn't understand New York."

I was undecided. If I stayed, I might get hurt. If I left, I was a coward.

My new boyfriend of a few months, Evan, who I'd met at Bar Lui, was a nice Jewish boy from the West Village. He gave me a sock with a few pounds of lead in it, which I carried around in my purse. I wasn't really sure how I'd be able to pull it out of my bag in time to stop an attacker; maybe I was supposed to walk down the block, swinging my athletic sock and whistling the theme song from *The Good, The Bad and The Ugly*? I didn't ask for an explanation, figuring that it might come in handy someday.

Meanwhile, the phone calls hadn't stopped, and it all came to a head when I went to the neighborhood police station. The severity of the calls was enough to warrant getting our phone tapped, and I soon learned that our stalker was calling from *inside* my building! After the police figured out where the calls were coming from, they encouraged me to file a restraining order and serve a subpoena for an appearance, which I did. Responding to the summons, an older, gentle-looking man showed up at the courthouse, claimed no knowledge of any calls, and suggested that it was probably his teenage daughter and her boyfriend who thought it would be funny to play a trick on Becky and me. And with that, the matter was closed.

When I'd decided to leave Angola, I'd wanted to return to New York and figure out a way to go to college—or at least a way to have goals bigger than to live in a place with clean water and diplomatic functions. Although I hadn't yet decided what path would be the right one for me, I knew I wanted more than what my daily existence in Angola had to offer. And yet, once I'd returned to New York, all of those plans were forgotten. I'd managed to survive two years of civil war in a country where bread and running water were scarce, and strangers with machine guns tried to get in my car—only to find late-night parties, a stalker, and a dangerous apartment on the Upper West Side. I had sought out the kind of recklessness in New York in an attempt to rival the perils I'd faced in Angola.

My existence had once again drifted—from making something of myself, to making sure I could swing my rent and have money left over for partying, while coping with the curveballs the city seemed to keep throwing at me. I had become increasingly distracted.

I had lost my way.

4

Bad Girl Gone Good

SOMETHING TURNED OVER INSIDE ME AFTER I HAD BEEN A year out of Africa. The late nights and the partying were taking a toll, and I simply began going out less and less. There was one significant motivating factor for the transition: I heard from Kim that Rhonda, the redhead who'd been our third roommate at our South Street Seaport apartment, had decided to go to college—a decision that effectively shook both Kim and me out of the haze of irresponsibility in which we'd been living for the past year.

Like us, Rhonda had graduated from Interlochen and gone to New York to fulfill her dreams of dancing on stage. Like us, she had also spent most of her time working in restaurants to make ends meet. Unlike us, Rhonda managed to take dance class at the same time and keep her head screwed on straight. Her decision to go to an academic college, as opposed to a school like Juilliard, was a breakthrough for me. It proved that dance wasn't the be-all-end-all career, a way of thinking that had been so ingrained in me during my years at a performing arts school. Over the last three years I had chosen to have absolutely no career when dance didn't work out for me rather than choosing a non-dance career. Apparently, Rhonda's step in that direction made Kim start evaluating her own life, too.

"I am going to apply to Columbia," Kim said nonchalantly a few days later.

Columbia? That was Ivy League. That's for people who are smart and go on to be doctors and lawyers. *That's not our kind of people*, I thought. Kim and I were so close, best friends as well as sisters, and yet, it was a decision she had made—a big one—without consulting me. I wasn't sure how to feel about it.

"Really? That's nice," I said. "How are you going to pay for it?"

"Mom and Dad have money," was her sanguine response.

I wasn't sure how serious she was. I knew she didn't have the money to pay the tuition for a school like Columbia, and it wasn't outrageous to assume that our parents would at least partially fund her college career if she decided to go after one. What surprised me, however, was that I took it so personally. We'd both been living independently since we'd graduated from high school, nearly four years earlier for Kim and three for me, and I couldn't believe that at twenty-two years old, Kim would take what I essentially saw as a handout from Mom and Dad— even if that handout would be willingly offered for a worthy investment that, in fact, a number of parents are happy to make for their children's future.

"Why can't you go to Hunter, a city college, like Rhonda?" I finally said. "That's affordable." How could she let our parents support her? How could that be okay with her? I had become fiercely independent by necessity and so had Kim. We had been on our own since we were teenagers, making our own decisions, financially self-sufficient, nobody to rely on but ourselves and each other. How could she want to change all that?

I considered the past year, one of working late nights in a restaurant, drinking and dancing into the wee hours, stumbling home, sleeping in late, and then starting the cycle all over again the next night. We had let New York transform us into voguish but tougher versions of ourselves—Kim, especially. She had become so cool and stylish. I wanted to be just like her. When she started wearing black all the time, I threw out my colorful tops and wore black, too.

"Why can't you girls wear a color?" my mother used to exclaim in her Filipino-accented English when we would go to Alaska to visit. "I guess we Alaskans are small-town; we are not 'chic.' Isn't that what you call it, 'chic'?"

Kim and I had spent a lot of time and money trying out the trendy new restaurants, getting into the coolest bars, and making friends with half the city's food and beverage industry. We were tough like my dad wanted us to be, but in New York City, that didn't mean putting up a tent in the pouring rain out in the bush; it meant dating without getting hurt, making friends with bartenders and managers, accepting gifts without commitment, free drinks and three-star cuisine, and moving on when people became boring or clingy. It was a way of life we'd sort of fallen into, and I was irritated that Kim now seemed willing to let our parents pay for college—what I considered her "indulgence." I never stopped to think about what a fine goal Kim had set for herself, or how much courage it had taken to consider applying to a top national university.

Then again, my competitive spirit had been honed after years of serious dance training, athletics, and trying to prove to my former-military, sportsman, survival-of-the-fittest father that I wasn't the squeamish type. I'd learned to shoot when I was eight, survived emergency water landings in Dad's prop plane, and late-night treks through the Alaskan wilderness to help butcher the moose he'd killed. I'd dealt with life in a Third World country decimated by an ongoing armed conflict, without friends or everyday conveniences. I was tough. I was unflappable. I was ultimately . . . bored.

Worse than that, I felt pretty damn empty inside. I knew I was capable of more than mixing drinks and dancing on bars—although I'd certainly enjoyed the lifestyle. In the back of my mind, though, was a nagging feeling that I'd regret it if I spent my life waiting for the big break that would make me famous as a model or dancer or some combination thereof. I wanted to make my own luck—and I needed to do it soon.

It occurred to me that college might be something I would find challenging . . . that I might even enjoy it. Hadn't going to college been one of the reasons I'd left Angola? How could I have forgotten? It was as if I finally remembered who I was, or at the very least, who I *wanted* to be. I needed to get my act together. The bartending, partying lifestyle was a dead end. Did I really want to spend the rest of my life dragging my skimpily clad self home from an all-night drinking and dancing session every morning? It had taken a casual relationship and a spur-of-the-moment move to Angola to pull me out of the downward spiral I'd managed to wedge myself into the first time I'd moved to New York. This time, there was no one but myself to rely on.

I consulted Becky, who stated wisely: "Kris, if you get accepted to Columbia, you will—*we* will—find a way for you to go." Somehow, I had managed to transition from being angry at Kim for thinking about applying to Columbia to wanting to apply to Columbia myself. I realized I'd been more upset that Kim was considering that step without me than I was truly worried about the fact that Mom and Dad would be helping to pay for it.

The more I thought about getting an education at Columbia, the more I thought, *Hell, if I get accepted to Columbia, I'm ready to accept whatever funds Mom and Dad want to give me.*

And Becky was right: I'd learned I could make things happen.

The apartment Becky and I shared on the Upper West Side, stalker and all, presented me with my first opportunity to be an advocate.

As the problems kept piling up—broken lock, no window, radiator gone wild—with absolutely no response from the managers of our apartment building, I began sending letters to management so that I had a record of each incident. Finally, Becky and I stopped paying our rent. There's nothing like a hit on someone's bottom line to garner immediate attention to a problem, and we promptly got sued. We landed in tenant/land-lord court, my first experience in a courtroom.

I'd saved copies of each letter I'd sent to request repairs and smugly handed them over to the judge during the hearing, shooting the landlord's lawyers my best don't-fuck-with-me look, á la Kim. Prior to our court date, we had consulted with Becky's uncle, a lawyer, who advised us to agree to pay at least some of the rent we owed. We couldn't talk him into accompanying us to court, but at least we knew what to expect. *You thought you could take advantage of us just because we're young,* I thought to myself. *Well, ha!* I mentally flipped the lawyers and the landlord the bird for added emphasis.

My roommate and I ended up with a settlement: The judge decided we only owed one month's rent instead of the three we would have paid, had our apartment not been neglected. The entire scenario was a very interesting experience for me, and one that made a lasting impression: Little people have leverage! Who knew? Somehow, a courtroom provided the environment where, ostensibly, all are created equal (as long as you keep records). Most significant, I learned that I found great comfort in the idea of achieving a resolution through the hearing of both sides of an argument. It brought me more satisfaction in my core than the rent reduction.

Standing up for myself made me brave enough to live on my own in the city. I moved (again) to Hell's Kitchen—and in 1988, it really *was* Hell's Kitchen. Throughout all of the landlord drama, I'd continued to investigate college opportunities. I knew I wasn't the typical college student, since I'd waited three years after graduating from high school to apply to college, and I knew it might take some creativity to be accepted to a prestigious school like Columbia. Nonetheless, I was determined to make my newfound college aspirations more than just talk. My research led me to Columbia's School of General Studies, which is a way for adult students who have taken time off between high school and college to attend Columbia University. Although I wasn't the typical General Studies student, either, being only a few years out of high school, it seemed like a perfect fit for me: The admissions counselors looked at more than just grades and SAT scores.

It wasn't an instant success. I was told to earn some college credits elsewhere and then to reapply. To prove that I could survive in the classroom, I enrolled in Borough of Manhattan Community College, where I took a four-class course load for my first semester. It was quite an experience—both exhausting and energizing—working in the bar until two a.m., trying to get home quickly so that I could get at least a little bit of sleep before my eight a.m. class the next morning. It was a grueling schedule, but with a little help from over-the-counter caffeine pills and my Alaskan-bred tenacity, I managed to earn straight As. And, at the end of the semester, I collected my transcripts, wrote my application essay, and reapplied to Columbia. This time, I was accepted. I was invited to start in the spring semester of 1989.

At first I was ecstatic, but then reality set in: *Oh, shit!* I thought. *How am I supposed to pay for this?* I'd worked my butt off bartending and taking classes at BMCC just to earn that acceptance letter; there was no way I'd let a little thing like money come between me and my shiny new college career. I took on a second job bartending at a music club called Woody's on the nights when I wasn't at Bar Lui, which eventually was sold to new owners and renamed Gonzales y Gonzales, where I picked up a few more shifts. I also took a shift or two at a restaurant called Wet Paint in SoHo, which, despite its bizarre name, managed to attract quite a few celebrities (I saw or served Gregory Hines, Paul Shaffer, David Byrne, Annie Lennox, and Jeff Goldblum, to name a few).

At first, I could only afford to take three classes per semester; with my three jobs, it was all I had time for, and I didn't have the cash to pay for more. I became a very dedicated student, rarely missing a class because I'd calculated the actual cost of each one. Kim and I took classes year-round to make up for not being full-time college students. (She'd found out about General Studies from me, earned some college credits at Hunter College, and applied and was accepted to Columbia, too.) We worked and went to school, trying to do well in both at the same time.

I loved going to a liberal arts college where I could take classes ranging from political science and history to women's studies and astronomy. It was a completely different educational experience from my high school years, which were so heavily focused on dancing. The professors at Columbia were amazing intellectuals with a range of ages and political leanings. While a few were boring, most were inspiring people who loved to teach the subject for which they had a passion.

One class in particular, History of the Sixties, made a huge impression on me. I learned about a period of upheaval when people wanted change; when they fought against oppression and were willing to ignore authority, to protest and fight for whatever they believed in. It was an eye-opener, giving me a glimpse into a time so contradictory to the one in which I was living—the early nineties—when everyone seemed happily complacent with their lives. This class would later influence my representation of the detainees at Guantánamo.

From the moment I walked through the stone-gated entrance on 116th Street, across Low Plaza, until the moment I graduated, I never took my college experience for granted. I knew I was getting a top-notch education and I was enjoying every moment of it. The majority of my fellow students had only been abroad with their parents; most of them had never had jobs. Their parents were lawyers or doctors. They'd gone to prep schools.

There weren't any lawyers in my family. I was the first person on my mom's side of the family to even go to college—and here I was, attending an Ivy League school.

I declared my major in my junior year: political science, with a concentration in political theory. I really enjoyed the combination of theory and real-world political affairs, and I'd chosen many of my political science classes for their international relations component. However, the one class I took at Columbia that ultimately decided my future was called Civil Rights and Liberties. It was part sociology and political science, part pre-law. In addition to learning about the substantive underpinnings of civil rights and liberties, we studied several well-known cases in depth, like *Brown v. Board of Education*, *NSPA v. Skokie* (the case about the right of neo-Nazis to march in Skokie, Illinois, a town made up of many Holocaust survivors), and *Brandenburg v. Ohio* (the famous First Amendment case). Reading those cases, I fell in love with the law. I realized that the law could create real change in people's lives, and that lawyers and judges were often the mechanism for that change.

I discovered that it wasn't about a president or a dictator passing laws, and all of those things presidents and dictators can do. By *practicing* law, you can change a society. You can protect your fellow citizens and your community against governmental intrusion. You can give individuals the freedom to live their lives the way they want to, and protect them from unfair treatment. I'd never known any lawyers (other than my brief encounter with Becky's uncle), but in an instant—or at least by the end of that semester—I was sure I wanted to be one.

5

Model Behavior

GRADUATION DAY IN MAY OF 1992 WAS A MAJOR HUSKEY celebration, not in small part because Kim and I were lucky enough to graduate together, with honors. My grandparents drove their RV all the way from their isolated mini-ranch in Texas to New York—and let me make this clear: They were not city people, having raised my dad and his brothers in Anchorage, Alaska, back when it was nothing more than a small town with more floatplanes than cars. My parents flew in from Alaska. Neither of my parents had gone to college—Dad had gone to flight school in Tacoma, Washington, and Mom to a Catholic nursing school in the Philippines.

It was what you might call a monumental moment for the Huskey family when my sister and I marched across the stage in blue caps and gowns at Columbia, especially considering that my parents had never really pushed Kim and me to go to college in the first place, and the time we'd spent partying between high school and college (not to mention my stint in Angola) had effectively convinced our parents that college wasn't in our futures. Frankly, this never seemed to bother our father, whose only requirement was that we "be the best we could be" no matter what we did. "Girls, you can be street sweepers for all I care. Just be the best goddamn street sweepers," he'd firmly say.

We had worked hard. We'd put ourselves through school—and succeeded. We'd loved every minute of it, and we turned out to be much more than street sweepers. We were proud of ourselves; I'd graduated Phi Beta Kappa (with the key-shaped, three-star-adorned charm to prove it) and *magna cum laude*; Kim had graduated *cum laude*.

I wasn't entirely sure what to do next. I'd considered several possibilities: law school, graduate school (to earn a Ph.D.), or something else entirely (perhaps trying my luck with modeling one more time). Before I'd graduated or had even taken the civil rights class that would so influence me during my senior year, I'd talked to Robert Amdur, a political science professor who had given me guidance on more than one occasion. I sought his advice on option two, getting a Ph.D. in political science, because I enjoyed school so much.

"What does that mean? What kind of job would I get?" I asked him.

"Teaching," Professor Amdur answered. "But it means another six to eight years of school, and no guarantee of a job while you're in school." He was trying to be encouraging while still giving me the hard facts.

Several more years of eating at Ollie's Noodle Shop, bartending, and scrambling to balance my checkbook? I couldn't take another six to eight years of moving from place to place, trying to find a cheap rent in a safe neighborhood, hoping the night's tips would cover my utilities for the month or food for the week. I had to come up with a better plan. That left me with law school or the something-else-entirely.

I was still working at Gonzales y Gonzales, but I decided to throw myself into modeling as a temporary career. At the very least it was a fun, easy way to make some money until I figured out what my next big career move would be. I managed to associate with a few agencies—both fashion and commercial—and I'd call them all first thing in the morning.

"Anything?" I'd ask.

"What's your name again? Let's see here . . ." was the response. "There's a call for brunettes; All-American look. What color are your eyes? Brown? No, they want green or blue. Call back tomorrow." Rejection once or twice is bad enough, and for a long time, every day I called, every agency I called, all I got was one rejection after another, anywhere from twelve to sixteen rejections a week. That's around sixty-four rejections in a month! To say I began to second-guess myself for thinking I could make even one dime modeling would be an understatement.

It was slow going at first; I was spending more time dropping in on various modeling agencies hoping someone would take an interest in me than I spent modeling. Most agencies have one day a week set aside for open calls where girls can walk in and meet with an agency rep in hopes of getting the agency to take you under its wing. At first I tried the big ones—Wilhelmina, Elite, Click—and when my luck ran out there, I moved on to second-tier agencies that seemed to like me when they first met me, though they would forget who I was or what I even looked like when I called in the morning for the day's listing of go-sees. A "go-see" is essentially a mini interview with the company that's looking for the model. You go and they see you. There is very little conversation. Eventually, the agencies began calling *me* each morning with a list of go-sees that had potential to pan out in my favor.

My days soon filled up with go-sees: traveling from company to company or designer to designer, trying on clothes, posing for a quick Polaroid, leaving my "card," and hoping they liked my look or the way I walked in their clothes. I started booking some work—mostly inexpensive clothing brands that you've never heard of—catalogs, trade newspapers, a few karaoke videos, a lot of showroom work for Zena jeans, and some regular gigs for a store called Bradley's in upstate New York.

Bradley's was good, lucrative work. I'd get a check for $125 each time after spending less than an hour with them. I'd be put in a chair, they'd do my hair and makeup, I'd put on some clothes, have my picture taken, and be off to the next go-see in no time.

I still bartended one or two nights a week as a backup, but it had become a lot tamer. We still danced on the bars, made good money, and had a few laughs. I'd built up a clientele at Gonzales y Gonzales, and it was a nice life—not because I made a ton of money or regularly splurged on extravagant items, but nice, as in *stable*. I wasn't coming home at odd hours, wondering where I'd been; I'd shed ten pounds just from cutting back on drinking; I felt completely and totally normal. After living in Saudi Arabia for a short period on account of my dad's piloting job with ARAMCO, being forced to move away from my parents when I was fourteen because there was no American high school on the ARAMCO compound, surviving my time in Africa, and my year of excess in Manhattan, normal was pretty damn nice.

My modeling career was starting to take off. Eventually, I became quite successful, earning about 75 percent of my income from modeling jobs. My ethnic look had set me apart from a lot of other aspiring models. Throughout my life, I had always gotten questions about my heritage because my looks were hard to pin down. People often made assumptions about me based solely on my looks, and although they were usually harmless, it made me realize just how dangerous it can be to make such judgments, as you often end up being wrong. The people who looked at me and saw an ethnic-looking Asian-type girl assumed (wrongly) that I wasn't American. It may seem harmless, but making assumptions about people based on their looks is, in many instances, considered discrimination. I was also reminded of that civil rights class I had taken at Columbia, where I learned about people that had been treated as less than equal simply because of their immutable characteristics. I tucked all this information away; I didn't know it then, but it would be very useful to me later.

I met a girl named Ana, another bartender at Gonzales y Gonzales. She was Filipino, too, but a lot more involved in her heritage than I'd ever been. My mother, who had come to this country at the age of twenty-one, had wanted my sister and me to be American, not Filipino. We didn't speak much of her native language. We had only visited her family in the Philippines once, and my sense of attachment to that culture was shaky at best. My friendship with Ana opened up a whole new world to me. She was proud of her Filipino background in ways that my mom had never taught me to be. My mom hadn't taught me to speak Tagalog (the main Filipino dialect); Ana's had. I didn't have many (actually, any) Filipino friends; Ana did. It wasn't that either way was better or worse; they were just different.

Ana introduced to me the Filipino community in Stuyvesant Town ("Stuytown"), a post–World War II, middle-income residential development, east of First Avenue and north of 14th Street. I met lots of young Filipino women who were hanging out with other Filipino women, talking about *pansit* (a Filipino noodle dish) and beauty pageants. I loved it. Soon I was part of the "Flips," and one day I found myself a participant in a Filipino beauty pageant. Me, a girl who had enough books on her shelves from women's studies courses at Barnard (taken during my days at Columbia) to be called a feminist (and proud to be one) in a beauty pageant! For my talent, I read the poem "For Strong Women" by Marge Piercy. I'm pretty sure I would have at least placed in the pageant if not for these few lines:

> A strong woman is a woman in whose head
> a voice is repeating, I told you so,
> ugly, bad girl, bitch, nag, shrill, witch,

ballbuster, nobody will ever love you back,
why aren't you feminine, why aren't
you soft, why aren't you quiet, why
aren't you dead?

My audience grew uncomfortably silent. They were probably hoping that I'd start twirling a baton rather than finishing the poem. When I did finish it, with an abrupt, "Thank you," there was a short smattering of applause. I'm sure they wondered what was going to come out of my mouth next, since I was obviously—gasp—a feminist.

Being a feminist in a beauty pageant was a little like being a socialist in America during the Cold War. I wasn't disappointed by the lack of enthusiastic approval; instead, I felt clever for coming up with such a powerful woman's voice at a beauty pageant, an emotion that was directly followed by embarrassment that I was naive enough to think anyone else would share my feelings.

Like any good feminist, I'd been giving a lot of thought to my career. I'd decided to start taking an LSAT (Law School Admission Test) prep course so that I could take the exam in December 1992. I wanted to be ready to apply to law schools for the following year, or the year after. My life became one of modeling, studying, and bartending—all in preparation for the next stage of my life. I was enjoying the modeling, but wasn't expecting it to make me famous.

I'd booked a job to model/dance in another music video that fall. It was a moderate-budget video for a group called

H-Town that had a look and sound a little like Boyz II Men—three young black guys with crooning voices and a little rap thrown in for good measure. We shot the video in a loft apartment somewhere in Brooklyn. There were two other models, a light-skinned black woman and an exotic-looking woman who turned out to be part South Asian and part black. I was in a chair getting my hair done, and the stylist, making conversation, asked me what my "other half" was.

"Filipino," I said without hesitation. I was used to this question.

"Oh, wow. Cool! Half Filipino and half African-American," the stylist said. And then I realized that the casting directors must've assumed I was at least partially African-American. Yet again, my ethnicity had been both an asset and a point of contention. I weighed my options and decided to come clean.

"Actually, I'm half Filipino and half Caucasian," I said. "I hope nobody blows my cover!" The stylist laughed and kept working.

The song was called "Knockin' Da Boots." It was the early nineties (thankfully), before thongs made a regular appearance in music videos, so although the clothes were skimpy, there wasn't as much skin as you see on MTV today. In the video, I wore a purple bra and panties and slunk out of a closet. It was a pretty intimate shoot—one of the guys in the group kisses my stomach, and there's a close-up of my lips blowing bubbles.

"See, Mom, those lips, those are my lips!" I said to my mom later, watching the video together, trying to distract her from the purple bra. Luckily for me, I have extremely supportive parents. My father was a hippie, and far from conservative, and my mother was just happy that her daughter had managed to graduate Phi Beta Kappa from Columbia.

It was a really fun shoot, although long, taking at least fourteen hours in all. No one on the set, not even the band, was famous (yet). I didn't have to do any acting; mostly just posing and slinking around in some skimpy outfit. I was supposed to be some hot chick wearing next to nothing, dancing around with pouty lips. The other two models were also hot chicks wearing next to nothing; for some reason, though, I got to wear less than their "next to nothing."

I knew a lot of models who had done a number of MTV videos, and there seemed to be a standard going rate: $150 for the whole shoot, no matter how long. Most of the videos didn't amount to much. But the H-Town video actually became very popular, and played on MTV all the time, eventually making it to MTV's Top Ten Countdown in 1993.

One night at Gonzales y Gonzales, a group of guys came in and immediately told me that I looked familiar. I shrugged, because that's just about the lamest pickup line in the book, but a few minutes later, it happened. "You're in 'Knockin' Da Boots'!" one guy yelled excitedly. "You're in the video on MTV! That's why you look so familiar." His friends hooted. "Yeah! I knew it was you!"

I couldn't believe it—I'd been recognized! These guys had seen the video enough times on MTV to recognize my face? (At least, I hoped it was my face and not my belly button they were recognizing.)

"Yeah," I said, ecstatic at being recognized. "That was me!"

There was the proof: I had done more than "arrive." I had made it! My modeling career was really starting to pick up, and at the same time, I was still planning on law school in a year or two. I hadn't expected to have to make a choice between the two, and I didn't think I had to at the moment, but my new boyfriend, who was also my LSAT tutor, threw a wrench in my grand plan to give "making it" one last shot. Doug was incredibly smart, intense, and passionate. He was also *very* edgy. Doug was thinking about applying to law school, too, but before he enrolled anywhere, he wanted to take a trip. He had never traveled overseas and wanted to go on a nine-month-long backpacking trip across Southeast Asia—and he wanted me to go with him.

I was torn: On the one hand, my modeling career was heating up, and I could probably make some really decent money if I stayed in New York just a bit longer. And then there was always the tiny little part of me that wondered, *What if? Maybe I'll get discovered; maybe I'll make it big . . .*

Around this time, I was asked to do another H-Town video for Luke Records. I also did an ad for a brand of tequila that was pretty popular on the West Coast, TQ Hot, and I booked a video commercial for L'Oreal shampoo. I was enjoying the work and the flexible hours, and I was keeping busy. Also, I'd already done a lot of traveling overseas. I knew that going away for a long trip would probably end my modeling career and force me to start down the lawyer road after our nine-month tour.

I'd made few friends in the modeling world: a roommate turned quasi-stalker named Dana, who seemed to be vying for the lead role in *Single White Female: The Sequel*. Most of the other models I met just didn't seem to think the way I did.

On the other hand, I'd recently started to see the ugly side of modeling. As a model, your every thought is about how you can improve your appearance. That's your job. I must've measured my waist every other day. (I had been guaranteed a two-week showroom job with a swimwear company if I could just get my waist down an inch, from twenty-seven to twenty-six.) I counted every calorie that went down my throat, trying to keep the total count below 1,750. I probably even counted calories that I only *thought* about eating.

I was incredibly hard on myself. I'd give myself a severe reprimand if I didn't get in a run each day, calculating what meal I would have to skip to compensate. I constantly thought about the clothes I was wearing, how my face looked, and whether I looked like what "they" wanted, whatever that was. It's a very self-centered existence, and that became clear to me the more time I spent at the events I was invited to through my agencies.

But after going to a few of them, I realized that most of the people I met were really rather boring. I was smart. Why weren't the other models smart? There were always exceptions, of course, but generally speaking, I rarely came across any. I came to the realization that when you're good-looking, especially if you're young, you don't need to be smart, or witty, or talented. People do things for you because you're pleasant to look at. If you grow up attractive, the teachers excuse your failings; your neighbors like you; you have friends; and you never really have to open your mouth. You succeed because you are pretty, not because you get straight As.

I realized that of the two—being smart and being pretty—I liked being smart more than I liked being pretty. It's not that I was offended if someone complimented my looks, but to be recognized for my smarts—well, that was something else entirely.

Being pretty, well, that was something I honestly wasn't used to. Sure, I had been a cute, Asian-looking baby, but soon thereafter I went through a very long "awkward stage," exacerbated by braces and unruly hair that never feathered quite like the other girls' hair. Even in high school, being pretty was certainly a good thing, but it only got you so far. The students at my performing arts high school were popular and successful because they were good at their art, whether it was music, dance, or drama—not simply because they had perfect smiles.

Not surprisingly, Doug was very persuasive. "Kristine," Doug coaxed, "let's go. Let's just pack up and go. You're tired of the whole superficial thing; you're planning on quitting and going to law school anyway. Come with me."

I sometimes wonder where I would've ended up if I'd stuck with it, but in the end, I chose Doug and adventure. Maybe I had wanderlust, or maybe I missed the excitement of living on the edge in Africa. Or maybe, I was just smitten with Doug. Doug was fun and spontaneous, but without trying to be cool, which seemed to be a ubiquitous characteristic in most people I met in New York. He was full of life and curious and passionate about almost everything, from ideas to sports to his relationship with me. We decided to apply to the same law schools and move together to our top choice after our trip.

I admired Doug for wanting to spend almost a year backpacking; for a guy who'd never been overseas, that was quite a commitment. Once I'd decided to go, it was full speed ahead. We spent the summer planning, asking Kim which places she'd liked best when she'd gone backpacking for a year in Southeast Asia. We bought a *Lonely Planet* guide and started reading, deciding which countries to visit and how much time to spend in each place, and we made a budget. Then we packed up our things, found sub-leasers for our apartments, applied to law schools (Stanford, Yale, Notre Dame, University of Texas, and a few others), and we were off in the fall of 1993.

6

Adventures in Backpacking

WE LEFT FOR INDONESIA IN NOVEMBER, PLANNING TO SPEND six weeks there, another six weeks in Thailand, then three weeks in Sri Lanka, a few months in India, and another month in Nepal. Then we'd go to Paris for three weeks until we returned to the U.S. in July 1994 to make our arrangements for law school. Neither of us had applied to a school in New York because living there was simply so expensive, and we both wanted to start our law school life in a totally new environment.

Yet again, my experiences in Angola came into play. I knew I needed very little to get by, and I very easily packed my backpack: a few necessary undergarments and toiletries that we might not be able to find in southeast Asia, one pair of shorts, a pair of leggings, two T-shirts, a dressy shirt in case we wanted to have dinner in a nicer restaurant, a pair of hiking sandals, and a pair of hiking boots. I'd buy a pair of cotton pants and a sweater when I needed them. We bought our airline tickets, trying to keep as much flexibility as possible, setting only the amount of time we planned to spend in each country. We made no plans for where or how we'd travel within each country, nor did we make any reservations for accommodations. We were going to be travelers, not tourists, beginning each day anew, acting spontaneously, ready to visit any town or site, wherever and whenever.

Every time we arrived in a new town, our first plan of action was to look for a place to stay so we could drop our packs, wash up, and explore. The goal was to find the cheapest, cleanest place to stay that had a private bathroom (very early on I decided we had to have *some* standards; otherwise, things could go downhill fast). Usually there was a "guesthouse" that met our needs—a cross between a youth hostel, a cheap bed-and-breakfast, and one of those independent motels off a major interstate that advertise rooms by the hour. We also quickly learned to actually look at the room before we agreed to take it. This served us well on many occasions, and soon, despite the best efforts of the proprietors, we had no problem saying, "Uh, no thanks, it's just too small," when, in fact, we wanted to say, "It smells like urine, underarm sweat, and curry in here." Disgusting!

A clean but sparsely furnished room with a private bath in a guesthouse was a mere $5 or $6 a night, sometimes less. Dinner of fresh fish—a splurge—could be had for $10 or $12. Usually we ate the local vegetarian rice or noodle dish for $2. We generally got around by walking, or, if we wanted to go farther away, to visit a tourist site or another town, we'd go by public bus or the various privately owned beat-up vans that seemed to run fairly regularly, though there were no published routes or timetables (the locals in Bali called them *bemos*). This made it tricky to figure out where they were going, and more than once, we ended up in a place completely different from where we wanted to be; we just got off, crossed the street, and took another one back in the same direction.

Time was never an issue for us, but money was: a ride on a bemo was only 10 or 25 cents. The "conductor" would hang out the open sliding door, one arm in the van, one arm waving, calling out the destination and upcoming stops. We affectionately termed them "bemo cowboys," because they looked like they were about to lasso another car or unsuspecting pedestrian as the van careened along like a wild horse.

In the morning, I would consult our trusty travel bible, *Lonely Planet*. "How about some temples today?" I'd ask.

"I don't want to do another temple; too many Westerners and Japanese tourists there, and people trying to sell you something," Doug said. We had just been to Besakih Temple in Bali, which was awe-inspiring, but so crowded with people that from afar it looked like an anthill swarming with camera-carrying ants wearing sun hats. "Let's get off the beaten path," he suggested.

"Okay," I said. "I'm game. Where to?" After consulting our guidebook more closely, we decided to take a ferry to a lesser-known island in the Indonesian archipelago, east of Bali, called Lombok.

We took two different bemos to a town just north of Malibu (Yes! Malibu, Indonesia), and piled onto a boat to reach the outermost island of three off the northwest coast of Lombok, called Gili Trawangan. The boat was small; we're talking a wooden, fishing-type boat, about twenty feet long, that probably seated fifteen people. The weather was pleasant as we were getting on the boat, but a swift, dark storm quickly made the situation serious.

"Here," Doug said, thrusting a raincoat—the kind that comes all folded up in a square packet the size of a tissue—at me. "Put this on." Of course, the rain was hitting the water and spraying up at us from below, so there was absolutely no way to keep from getting drenched—and yet, I figured a raincoat couldn't hurt. I wriggled into mine and helped Doug into his, hoping the lightning would cease.

"Well, we're off the beaten path!" I said grimly, surveying the faces of the natives who were our only fellow travelers. "This is certainly spontaneous and exhilarating. The natives look just overjoyed."

Suddenly, the wind picked up, the rain got even more violent—and the natives started to pray. Doug and I joined in, recognizing the sounds of prayer even though we didn't speak their language. Then the unspeakable happened: Someone jumped out of the boat. We couldn't see the island through the storm, but we'd gotten close enough that we could wade to it—had to, really—wearing our (completely useless) raincoats and toting our backpacks high over our heads. We'd made it. Barely.

Once the weather cleared, we were glad we'd braved the boat ride. Just as *Lonely Planet* had promised, the island was spectacular, and tourist-free. "Not for the faint of heart," the guide read, "but well worth the trip." We agreed 100 percent. It was a tiny little island, practically in the middle of nowhere, and you could walk the entire circumference in two hours.

The ride to our next destination in Lombok was not quite as traumatic as the trip out to Gili Trawangan had been, unless you count the third leg of the trip, which came after the boat ride off the small island and the bus trip inland to a bigger town. For this leg, each of us jumped up behind a local on a motorbike to make our winding way to a village in the mountains, our backpacks perilously redistributing the weight every time we took a turn. *WE'RE GOING TO TIP OVER! WE'RE GOING TO TIP OVER!* I screamed inside my head while smiling placidly at the driver when he turned around to check on me.

Finally, we made it to Bangkok. We did the usual: scouted places to stay, figured out which ones were the cheapest, and booked a room. *Cheap* was always the most important factor; relatively clean was another factor, but I stress the word "relative" here. We dropped our bags and I went to find a phone— I wanted to check in with my parents, and also call my sister to ask if I'd gotten any acceptance letters for law school yet. (I hadn't.) My parents, however, had remembered a friend of theirs who was living in Bangkok, a pilot named Bob Archer who'd lived in our basement in Alaska during his hippie years and who had flown with my dad in Saudi Arabia for ARAMCO as well.

"I told Bob you'd be in Bangkok, and he told me to give you his number," my father said, proud of himself. "You should call him tonight and see if you can meet up with him—I'm sure he could give you the local's tour."

The local's tour was exactly what we were looking for. I thanked Dad and dialed Bob's number. He answered on the second ring.

"Hi," I said. "It's Kris Huskey, Pete's daughter. Remember me?"

"Kristine!" Bob said softly. I could hardly hear him over the cacophony of Bangkok's main rail station, which was right next door to our digs. "I'm so glad you called! I'll be flying out tonight, but I'll be back tomorrow afternoon—how about dinner? Tell me where you're staying and I'll pick you up."

I gave him the address: "Uh, near the train station and in a run-down building with a lopsided sign that says 'Happy Traveler's Inn.' "

When Bob showed up, he took one look at our "happy" inn and made other plans.

"Get your stuff," he said. "We're leaving."

Doug and I looked at each other and blinked.

"What?" I managed to squeeze out. "We're paid up through the weekend. It's not *that* bad." We knew it wasn't the Comfort Inn, but we were on a budget. It hadn't seemed like such a bad place when we decided to stay there, but now I looked at it again, trying to see it through Bob's eyes. Okay, so the place was . . . dirty; a run-down hotel. And yes, it was gross and scary, even. But so what? It was in our price range, and we didn't have much room for bargaining. Plus, we'd been exhausted when we finally got to Bangkok, and this place seemed as good as any.

Bob, however, was having a harder time seeing the place's charms—or else he knew something about it that we didn't know. "Don't worry about the money," he said. "You two can stay with me."

We grabbed our things—a process that only took five minutes—and went to dinner with Bob and his girlfriend, Nina, only our second time eating in a real restaurant since we'd left New York. The first had been a Christmas meal of Indonesian food in Bali. Bob and Nina paid the bill—it came to almost $25! I couldn't believe it. Doug and I had been eating from the street stalls where we could get a bowl of noodles for 50 cents, with some chili pepper thrown in for free.

"I've got an extra bedroom," Bob said over his noodles. "It's in a gated community, and you'll be a lot safer there."

We didn't argue. It had occurred to both of us that staying at Bob's probably meant we'd be able to take the first hot showers we'd had in weeks. Bob could've lived in a cardboard box for all we cared; as long as it was cheap and had hot water, we were sold.

Bob's apartment was, in fact, much better than a cardboard box. He gave us a spare key, and we used his place as a base to travel around Thailand. It was such a relief, not having to carry everything we owned on our backs everywhere we went. Heading south, we went to the tiny island of Ko Pha Ngan, home of the famous Haad Rin Full Moon Parties, then Ko Tapu, otherwise known as James Bond Island, where *The Man with the Golden Gun* was filmed. We spent the night in a Muslim fishing village built on stilts above the water, where nobody had running water, but everyone had TVs.

We eventually went to the city of Chiang Mai, which is the jumping-off point for trekking in mountainous northern

Thailand and exploring its caves. Our time in the north was a series of treks, with beautiful vistas and river caves, interrupted by comical transportation struggles. From Chiang Mai, we took an open-air truck with benches in the back that our guidebook had recommended; in fact, it was the only way to get to Pai, short of renting our own car. The truck lurched from side to side as it wound its way up the mountainside. The drive was notorious for making people sick; curvy roads combined with bouncy, rickety seats makes for a lot of upset stomachs. And sure enough, just as *Lonely Planet* had described, there they were—little plastic bags hanging off the sides of the truck in case one's stomach couldn't handle the bumps. This was equal opportunity nausea: Local or foreign, it didn't matter where you were from, you were almost certainly going to be sick.

"I don't care if I ever eat again," I said as Doug helped me climb down from the truck. Neither of us had proved immune to motion sickness, and we were both still a little green. Fortunately, neither of us had had to resort to the baggies.

"I know what you mean," Doug replied. "Why did we come all the way up here again?"

I consulted our guidebook. "Tham Lod," I said. "*Lod* means cave and *Tham* means . . . well, I guess that's just the name of the place. It's a river cave, with stalactites and stalagmites, and seventeen-hundred-year-old coffins. And three hundred thousand swifts return to the entrance of the cave in the evening. Wow, that's a lot of bird shit." I kept reading. "We need a guide to take us in a wooden boat with a petrol lamp. Cool!"

"Right," he said.

During the tour of Tham Lod, we met a lawyer. He wasn't a tourist, but he wasn't your usual backpacker, either. He had a backpack and looked hardened, but not frazzled or all that gritty like the rest of us. He must've been staying in some more-upscale guesthouses. I was thrilled to discuss our plans for law school with him. Our newfound friend, on the other hand, was positively not thrilled about the practice of law, which he had been doing in a big law firm after graduating from Stanford (my dream school!). He described it succinctly: "Long hours, boring, restrictive, oppressive, boring—did I say that already?" And he must have used the phrase "It sucks!" at least three or four times.

Doug and I had had several discussions about law school during our trip. Although he seemed to be losing interest, I was still determined to go. I'd promised myself that I would go no matter what Doug ultimately decided. The attitude of this lawyer-turned-cave-explorer only helped fuel Doug's developing negativity toward it.

All the while, I was desperate to find a phone so that I could get news from home. When I did come across a phone, conversations often panned out the same way.

"Hi, Kim!" I'd say into the receiver, louder than I'd intended and betraying my anxiety to know if any acceptance letters had come in yet. "Any news?" I was anxious to hear from Stanford, and Kim was always very sensitive when delivering the bad news.

"Nothing new this week, Krissy," she'd say. "But I'm sure something will come tomorrow, since you're calling today."

Our next stop was Sri Lanka, where we had planned to spend three weeks; however, after just a few days of erratic bus and train schedules and dirty, neglected tourist sites, we left Sri Lanka early to make our way to India.

"What should we do today?" I asked Doug again over breakfast. It was our third day in India and I was scanning *Lonely Planet*. Mornings were a really stressful time of day for us, with so many decisions to make. Every day was a test: of our mental stamina, our health, our survival skills, our patience with each other. There were no set routines. Each day we had to figure out how to get where we wanted to go (after we figured out *where* we wanted to go), and then, once we reached our destination, there was a whole new list of decisions to be made—where to stay, how to get around, where to find food.

Doug hadn't answered. I looked up from the guidebook to see him looking around, soaking it all in, taking long sips of his coffee. He hadn't even heard me. It wasn't anything new. I'd somehow taken on the role of tour guide during our months of travel, and until this point, I hadn't really minded. That day, however, I realized how stressed out it was making me to always be in charge, and I resented Doug's ability to let me lead the way while he just sat back and enjoyed the view.

There we were, on the brink of a major life change, enjoying our last months of freedom before plunging back into the challenging world that is law school, with a career to follow that would certainly be just as challenging. Or at least *I* was enjoying *my* last few months of freedom; it was starting to look more and more like Doug didn't want to go to law school. For now, though, we were living in the moment—moments that, for me, were an occasion to rise to a challenge, but for Doug seemed to be an occasion to relax while I did all the work. It didn't bode well for us as a couple, to be able to function in the real world of stressful situations, but we loved each other, we were on our great adventure, and at the time, that was all that mattered.

India is, in a few words, crowded, dirty, and poor. But at the same time, it is also eye-opening. When you travel for nearly a year on a very limited budget, and you realize the people in the places you visit are living on budgets that don't even come close to the limited amount you've set for your trip, you can't help but feel that you are extraordinarily lucky.

We saw and did all of the beautiful, exotic things that are India—the Ajanta Caves with the ancient paintings, the Taj Mahal, the palaces in Rajasthan, Jaisalmer Fort, monoliths in Mahabalipuram, the colorful markets full of spices and bangles, the erotic temple of Khajuraho. We ate curry morning, noon, and night; we went on safaris, even getting within twenty-five feet of a wild tiger on the back of an elephant. We took a three-day camel trek through the desert, sleeping outside; our bed was out under the moon and the stars on a soft carpet of sand, in a rented, worn-out, slightly smelly sleeping bag, which, by then, didn't even bother me. We rode train after train, bus after bus, for hours just to see a fascinating sight, like a giant twenty-foot-tall stone bull with garlands. We made friends and shared food with strangers, Westerners and Indians alike. It was all glorious and terribly exhausting. *Lonely Planet* calls it "clamorous sensory overload," and it was.

We ended our backpacking experiences on a high note—literally. We'd decided to backpack through the Himalayas in Nepal, on a route that was on most backpackers' lists: the Annapurna Circuit.

In the first ten days, we walked nine or ten hours a day, increasing in altitude each day. The higher we went, the colder it got, and at around thirteen thousand feet, the hiking became more challenging because the air was thinner. By the time we got to Thorang Phedi, also known as Thorang High Camp, at 4,900 meters (just over 16,000 feet), we were only hiking a few hours a day. It was terrifyingly cold when the sun set, and the night before we crossed over Thorang La-Pass—the most difficult portion of the trek—I put on every article of clothing I'd brought with me: stretch pants, cotton pants, turtleneck, and my newly acquired sweater and hat, and climbed in my sleeping bag for the night. *How cold was it going to get another 1,700 feet up?* I couldn't bring myself to say it out loud. I wondered if I would survive the pass to descend back to normal temperatures.

The next day, we woke at four a.m. in order to get across the most difficult part of the pass before the high winds typical of later in the day made it impossible. It started snowing almost as soon as we set out. There was already snow on the ground, the air was thin, and it was all I could to do focus on putting one foot in front of the other. It was incredible, this amazing physical feat. You think, *I can't do it, I can't do it . . .* and then you realize you've taken twenty more steps. We finally made it, reaching the top of the pass at 5,416 meters (17,764 feet), nestled between two icy mountains. We were with a few other trekkers we'd been hiking with the last week or so, two hearty Australian brothers. We hooted and hollered, took pictures. We'd survived, losing about ten or twelve pounds in three weeks, but gaining some friends for life, and amazed at what our bodies were physically capable of.

When we were finished with our trek, we were ready to return to civilization, to face the reality of the decisions we'd made on long bus rides in between the small towns of India. I'd had to make my law school decision right in the midst of our travels; if you don't accept by a certain date before the academic year, they'll give your spot to someone else. I figured that I'd waited long enough to postpone what I really wanted to tackle next.

My life-altering phone conversation with my sister had occurred in India, somewhere in between visiting the Taj Mahal and going on a tiger safari.

"Kim! It's Kris," I said, the sense of urgency in my voice immediately apparent. "The acceptance letters have to be there by now. What's the verdict?"

"Well, Krissy, I have some good news and I have some bad news," she began. "The bad news is that you weren't accepted to

Stanford. The good news is that you have your choice between a pretty hefty scholarship to Notre Dame, a full scholarship to a law school in Chicago, and you were accepted to the University of Texas at Austin." She hesitated. "What about Doug?"

What about Doug? I wondered. It was becoming clear that Doug didn't want to go to law school after all, and although he would wait to reveal his decision until we'd reached our final Parisian destination, I already felt betrayed. We'd been talking about getting married, and I'd thought we had our futures planned out, at least for the next few years: law school, marriage, becoming lawyers together.

"Doug is . . ." I hesitated, ". . . probably not going to law school." There was a brief pause. "Apparently, he's missing his friends too much to leave them again for law school."

Kim quickly changed the subject. "So when are you coming back to New York?" she asked.

"Not for another two months. We have Nepal, and then the two weeks in Paris," I said, "but as soon as I get back, I'll be packing up and moving out." Then I added emphatically, more to myself than to my sister, "I don't care what Doug's doing—*I* am going to law school."

Part II: Life Now

7

Finding My Passion

NEVER RENT AN APARTMENT YOU HAVEN'T SEEN IN PERSON, I thought, opening the door to my new place in Austin. It was the first lesson I'd learned in law school, before classes had even started. I'd left New York in a flurry of packing, shipping, and good-byes—to Doug, to Kim, to my friends—and I'd chosen an apartment, sight unseen, through a real estate catalog advertising apartments for rent. I found when I arrived in Austin that I'd managed to select an apartment in the worst part of town. *Am I forever destined to make bad apartment choices?* I wondered.

Not one to give up when the going gets tough, I stuck it out—for a while, at least. I couldn't imagine that anything in Texas could possibly be as bad as Hell's Kitchen, or give me half of the troubles I'd been through in New York. The last thing I needed was more landlord drama when I was trying for a (somewhat) fresh start.

Leaving Doug had been hard. He hadn't completely closed the door on law school; instead, he'd decided to defer his enrollment at the University of Texas for a year. To him, it was no big deal. To me, it felt like certain death for our relationship. I still felt betrayed and hurt. We'd spent so much time planning our future together; how could he just change his mind?

I had chosen UT because at the time, its law school was ranked twelfth in the nation—the highest-ranking school to which I'd been accepted. Add to this the fact that tuition was less than $15,000 per year, even for out-of-state students (which, in comparison to similarly ranked law schools like Georgetown, Duke, or NYU, was a total bargain), and the fact that it was in Austin, which I knew was a fun city, choosing UT was an easy decision.

I sighed, surveying my crummy apartment in its crummier neighborhood, half grimacing, half smiling. I had moved to Austin, and it felt right. Law school felt right. Doug still felt right, too. I refused to overthink it. I was taking our relationship one day at a time.

In the meantime, I got settled into my new town. Once I cleaned it up, the apartment wasn't so bad, but the neighborhood was rough. The neighbors were rougher. After a couple months of brazen stares and low whistles every time I walked through the apartment complex, and struggling to get my reading done while surrounded by the sounds of drunken revelry, fistfights, and sirens, I'd had enough. I went to see UT's tenant-landlord service for students, for help in evaluating my options. The news wasn't good; I was told Texas is not "tenant-friendly." This notion was a new one to me, as New York is rather tenant-friendly. (I would soon discover a number of differences between Texas and New York, and its tenant/landlord laws were just the tip of the iceberg.) Basically, I'd have to break my lease, pay one or two months' rent until the apartment was re-rented, and forfeit my deposit. I wasn't about to just forfeit that kind of cash, at least, not until I developed a new "friend" in the complex. He came by one Friday night on his way out for a night of partying (though it appeared and smelled like he'd started his night hours before), to ask if I wanted to join him.

"Um, no, thanks. I'm really busy studying," I responded, trying to be neighborly and at the same time remember what subject I was supposed to be studying, while thinking, *Please go away and don't pick up on the fact that I live here alone.* My friendly neighbor came by a few more times late at night, and each time I tried to respond nicely but firmly.

"No, thanks. Really, that's okay, I should study."

And another time: "Boyfriend? Yes, I have a boyfriend. He's, um, out. But I'm sure he'll be back soon."

Frankly, I was afraid my "friendly" neighbor would eventually get aggressive and try to push his way into the apartment. I wasn't scared, but I was nervous.

After a week of the late-night invitations, I started looking for a new apartment. I lucked into a place fairly close to campus—Oak Park Apartments, right in the quirky Hyde Park neighborhood—my first long-term home. I couldn't believe the rental prices in Austin; compared to what I had been used to in New York, they were dirt-cheap. I rented a huge one-bedroom apartment with a full kitchen, separate dining room, and a walk-in closet. I felt like a millionaire, even if the carpet was a little weary.

It certainly made an impression on Kim, who'd lived in closet-sized New York apartments longer than I had. She'd assumed I was joking or exaggerating when I described my new place, but when she came to visit the first time, she finally realized the difference between life in NYC and life pretty much anywhere else.

"Here we are," I said, sweeping my hand in a circle to show off the full view. "Home sweet home, Texas-style."

"Oh my God, Krissy!" Kim shrieked. "Wow. This is practically a mansion. Look! You have a full kitchen! And look at the size of your bedroom! Wait, you have a separate bedroom! And your walk-in closet is bigger than my kitchen. How can you afford this?"

"Kim, my rent is five hundred a month," I said to her unbelieving face. "I swear. Six hundred and fifty square feet. Welcome to life outside Manhattan. And, P.S., my *bathtub* is bigger than your kitchen."

"If I could ever bring myself to leave New York, I guess I could have a place like this . . . and all I do is boil water, remember?" she said. After ten years in the city, Kim had become a true New Yorker. I doubted she'd ever leave. She had quickly left the publishing business she went into right after graduating from Columbia and was back in the restaurant business making her way up the chain of command, where she would ultimately become general manager in some of the most popular and prestigious restaurants in New York.

"How's school?" she asked. "Is it as hard as everyone says? Is it boring?"

Is it ever, I thought. Hard, not boring—at least most of the time. In truth, while I hadn't thought law school would be a piece of cake, I really hadn't expected it to be quite so difficult. Like every other law student, I'd read attorney/author Scott Turow's *One L*, a description of his experience as a first-year law student at Harvard Law School ("1L" is law school code for first-year law student; a 2L is second-year law student; 3L is third-year). Also like every other law student, I'd thought it wouldn't be so hard for *me*. I mean, I was top of my class at Columbia; didn't that count for something? Duh. I soon came to realize that every student attending a good law school got there because they were at the top of their classes as an undergrad.

But somebody has to be in the bottom half, and honestly, I think no matter where you are, law school is hard, plain and simple. At UT, in your first year, you take six courses (contracts, civil procedure, property, criminal law, constitutional law, and torts), all of which are required. My year (class of 1997), the incoming class was divided into five sections of about a hundred to a hundred and twenty-five students each. I ended up in Section Three. I took all six first-year courses with my Section Three compatriots, and in every class, the students are seated alphabetically in the same configuration. So you end up not only taking three or four classes a day, five days a week, with the same hundred people; you also have to sit next to the *same person every day* for a whole year!

Stress breeds either bonding or homicidal intentions, and the first year of law school can be extremely stressful. Brandon Hudgeons, a boot-wearing, chicken-fried steak-eating Texas boy from Midland, sat immediately to my right, day in and day out. Brandon had been a creative writing major at Dartmouth and had read as many books as I had, including poetry, so he wasn't really the stereotypical Texan that he tried hard to portray. We shared many a silent laugh in class, and only once or twice did I want to kill him, primarily because he was so relaxed while the rest of us were perpetually stressed out. To this day, I remain close friends with the other "H" students who sat near me in Section Three: Brandon, Michael Hill, and Trent Howell. In fact, one of my non-H friends from law school who hung out with us—Laura Blood (who would later marry Michael Hill)—was introduced on more than once occasion as "a friend of the Hs."

In each class, you'd be assigned about twenty to thirty pages of reading in preparation for the next day, making for an average of sixty, sometimes ninety pages of reading a night. Even for an avid reader like me, that was just a shitload of reading. However, true to my A-student self, I did the reading. All of it. And I went to every class, unlike some of my classmates. I was motivated both by the fear of getting called on in class and the need to get my money's worth—I was, after all, paying for school through various student loans and minor scholarships.

Law school classes can be intimidating. I had gotten used to large class sizes at Columbia, but in law school, the students file in and sit down in their assigned seats (next to their alphabetical neighbors), and then the professor enters, jumping right in. They expect you to have done the reading, and usually begin classes with a series of questions about the previous night's material, calling on names at random from their seating chart.

"Personal jurisdiction," Professor Issacharoff said in his blunt, East Coast manner. "Ms. Huskey, what were the facts in *Worldwide Volkswagen*?"

"Um, World . . . wide . . . Volks . . . wagen," I responded, drawing out the name, racking my brains for the details of this one particular case from among numerous others I had stayed up reading until two in the morning. "Well, there was an automobile involved . . ."

If you didn't know the answer when called upon, one of two things would happen: You would either guess and get the answer right, uttering a temporary sigh of relief until the professor came after you with a follow-up question (producing more sweat and chills) or moved along to the next victim (and you thanked your lucky stars); or you would guess wrong (not giving an answer was not an option), and then wait for the ridicule/sarcasm/disappointment/example-making that followed.

In torts class one day: "Is that your answer, Ms. Huskey? In what world does it make sense for the plaintiff to receive triple damages for his contributory negligence?" I could hardly understand what language Professor Robertson, our torts guru, was speaking, but I knew I'd given the wrong answer. After an exchange like that, you'd be sure to do your reading before the next class.

After a week or so at UT, I figured out the key to surviving law school: Ask questions. It sounds simple, right? It hit me during my contracts class with Professor Weintraub, a character right out of a law school movie, the '90s version of *The Paper Chase*. Now that I am a professor, too (more on that later), I realize that much of teaching is really a performance, the goal being to keep your students interested and active participants, if not simply to keep them awake. Each morning, to start his class, Professor Weintraub would stride down the steps to the front of stadium-configured classroom, wearing his polyester suit from the seventies and thick black-framed glasses. He'd toss the small wooden podium off the front table onto the floor (loudly), throw his leg on the end, bend his knee, and stretch like an athlete about to start a serious workout. It was an intimidation tactic—the noise, the stretching—and it worked.

After the stretch, he'd boom: "Any questions?" For the first few days of class, there were none, which would leave Professor Weintraub free to pull out his seating chart and call on someone in order to grill him or her on a case, or a particular Latin phrase, which are freely scattered throughout American case law.

"Assumpsit?" He inquired on the first day of class. "What does *assumpsit* mean?" There were no volunteers. "Anyone on murderer's row?" Weintraub asked, looking up at the back row. "Didn't anybody read this case? Didn't anybody look this word up, or does everybody here speak fluent Latin?"

Professor Weintraub also had a collection of non-Latin phrases he'd yell out from time to time, hoping to make some dry principle in contract law meaningful: "You can't unscramble the eggs!" he'd call out. After a few days of intimidating questions about Latin phrases and terms like "consideration" (not what nice people do for other people), it hit me: If I came prepared with a few questions to ask at the beginning of class (carefully researched, certainly, but on my own terms), maybe I could avoid being called on at random while he was teaching. I tested my theory over the next few days, asking a question at the beginning of each class. It worked—Weintraub never called on me—and it became a tactic I employed in all of my classes throughout law school.

My fellow students were mostly straight out of undergrad, which they'd entered straight out of high school. At twenty-seven, I was studying with other students who were four or five—sometimes six—years younger than me. Being older and more experienced than most of my classmates did have its advantages. I had faced so many obstacles, put myself through Columbia and graduated with honors, traveled abroad, lived in New York and Africa; not a whole lot actually scared me. And when it did, I could put up a pretty good front. Law school was intimidating, true, and so was Professor Weintraub (and most of my fellow Section Three members were afraid of Issacharoff, too), but I didn't back down. My good friend Laura Blood later told me that she had been afraid of *me* because I used to "talk back" to our professors. Talk back? *Me?* I would never do something like challenge an authority figure. . . . Right.

Our property professor, Chambliss, was an easy target. She hadn't been teaching that long, and her lack of confidence often showed. It was easy to let your mind wander during her class. One day, Brandon and I were doing a *New York Times* crossword puzzle together in class (yes, in class), and the ink in his pen seemed to run dry. Brandon shook the pen, which then unloaded its ink all over him. He looked at me unknowingly, smiling with blue spots all over his face, looking like a Dr. Seuss character. I couldn't stop my shoulders from shaking as I tried to control my laughter. Chambliss chose to ignore us. Another day in property class, my daydreaming was interrupted by Professor Chambliss: "What does the dissent say, Ms. Huskey?" (The "dissent" is the judge or judges who disagree with the majority opinion in a case.)

"I've got to read it first," I replied.

"You can't say that *out loud*," Chambliss replied. The class chuckled, not too quietly; if it had been Issacharoff, you would have heard gasps of surprise at my audacity, and probably a little snickering. Personally, I think that's why Issacharoff took to me and became my mentor; he appreciated anybody who stood up to him.

Another memorable student in my class was Clark Richards, son of former Texas governor Ann Richards. Clark was what we called a "gunner"—the student whose hand immediately shot into the air anytime a professor asked a question. Some of us had a lot of affection for him, while others just found him annoying. In truth, Clark *was* exhausting. He was so passionate about the law, about his classes, that inevitably, a conversation with him would turn into an in-depth discussion of the topic at hand. In class, though, we were all entertained by him. Our professors would ask a question and Clark's hand would shoot up like a rocket, taking the focus off the rest of us, even if only for a split second.

"There are two ways to approach an exam question," Professor Robertson once said to Clark about his exams. "The first is to nail it precisely with a twenty-two. The second is to spray it with a shotgun. You, sir, are the latter."

But that wasn't the only thing about Clark that had the rest of us rolling our eyes; he also had a laptop computer that went everywhere with him. This may not seem particularly noteworthy today, when most colleges require students to bring their laptops to class, but in 1994, having a laptop—let alone dragging it with you to every class—was quite a novelty. While we all found Clark interesting for one reason or another, we also thought he was a dork. A quirky, passionate dork, sure, but a dork just the same. This is ironic for a variety of reasons, in no small part because, let's face it—we were all dorks. We spent our free time studying. When midterms and finals came around, we'd spend six or eight hours a night, ten or twelve on the weekends, studying together. (There were even study groups, and they could be real clique-ish, as in "What study group are you in?" being met with disdain or approval depending on the answer.) It was a far cry from my years of hard partying in NYC.

One Friday night, I was studying contracts with my best friend, Megan Alter (who would later go on to marry Brandon Hudgeons). Megan and I had been thrown together in another required grouping within Section Three, the "TQ." A TQ (teaching quizmaster) was a group of ten or twelve students led by a third-year law student. We went to a lot of social events together (as if we were freshmen back in college), and it was an immediate source for study partners. Megan and I were in the same TQ and sized each other up pretty quickly. She was physically the opposite of me—small and blonde, from Fort Worth, with a thick Texas accent—but she was my compadre in style and street smarts. She didn't take crap from anybody; she was very direct (I think she was really a Yankee masquerading as a cowgirl); and she had worked her way through college as a waitress, then had spent a year or so in a real job before going to law school. The thought of studying in a larger group of twenty-three-year-olds didn't excite either of us, so Megan and I studied together, just the two of us.

That night, we pulled out our contracts books, going through each case methodically, discussing the dissent ad nauseam, alternately firing questions at each other, and typing up our notes on our own laptops (yes, we had laptops, but we weren't so dorky as to bring them to class). After about six hours of the "Hairy Hands" case, "consideration," and the Uniform Commercial Code (UCC), Megan looked up at me, weary. "I don't think I can do this anymore," she said. "My brain's stopped working. It's Friday night. Do you think anybody else in our section is studying this much on a Friday?"

Truthfully, Megan was probably tired of disagreeing with me over the meaning and impact of FOB ("Free On Board," a contracts term, something Weintraub had asked us to explain), and she had too much class to tell me I was painfully, annoyingly contrarian.

"Yes," I replied. "More. Clark is probably footnoting his footnotes. But I hear you. Why don't we take a break, reward ourselves? I think I have beer in the fridge." This was remarkable, because I didn't even like beer.

"Great idea!" Megan responded enthusiastically.

I got up and rummaged through the refrigerator. "I have . . . um . . . a couple of Miller Lites. Sound okay?"

"Sounds good," Megan said.

"But let's not go crazy, okay? Let's just split one." I replied, cracking open our shared beverage and pouring two half glasses. "Cheers!"

Let's not go crazy and have a whole light beer each? Now, that would be excessive. Times had obviously changed.

We studied. We made eighty-page study outlines. We memorized cases and recited what they stood for to each other, over and over again. The details seemed like such minutiae that at times I completely forgot why I had been so passionate about law in the first place. Reading Con Law cases (as in law of the Constitution) sometimes reminded me, but the long opinions also helped me fall asleep at night when I had consistent insomnia.

In law school, your first year pretty much decides your future as a lawyer. Even though those classes rarely come back to haunt you down the road (when your experience counts for more), initially, it's all about your first year. Those grades are the ones you use to get a job during the summer after your first and second years of law school.

During spring semester of my first year, I sent letters to all the well-known public interest–related organizations in New York. I applied to the NOW Legal Defense and Education Fund. I applied to a number of nonprofit organizations, including Volunteer Lawyers for the Arts and several others I'd never heard of but that sounded civic-minded. In law school, I was a tough chick from NYC with a wardrobe full of mini-skirts, combat boots, and a black motorcycle jacket, engendering many stares and some giggles from my mostly Texan classmates. *Of course* I wanted to work in public interest; after all, it was a civil rights course during my undergrad years that had inspired me to go to law school in the first place. Unfortunately, I was having a hard time *finding* any opportunities, let alone applying for them. In the 1990s, UT Law School was really focused on helping their students land jobs with law firms; the public interest side of law was pretty neglected. If you were interested in furthering the public good, you were pretty much on your own.

Finally, after applying to several organizations in New York, where I was planning to spend the summer, I realized I wasn't going to be able to make this happen on my own. I needed help. I sought out UT's Career Services Office (CSO), and explained that I was hoping to land a public interest job, ideally working with civil rights issues, women's rights in particular. (Oh, Filipino beauty pageant, where are you now?)

"You know," my counselor began, "we have a program for minority students. Basically, you take a writing test and have to meet a minimum undergrad GPA requirement, which I see that you do. It's a partnership with various law firms. They look at your résumé in an attempt to get more minority students into law firms for the summer. There's no guarantee that you'll get a job, of course, but it's a great way to get your résumé in front of a lot of law firms, with a guarantee that they'll at least look at it."

I hesitated: The law firms in this program were definitely not in my target group. I had gone to CSO for advice on public interest jobs, not big, evil, corporate law jobs.

"If a law firm wants to hire you, Kristine," my counselor continued, more gently, obviously noticing my hesitation, "wouldn't it be a terribly wasted opportunity not to take it? It's really good money. You might as well check it out and make your decision after you see what opportunities are out there."

"But I really don't want to do corporate law stuff," I responded. I wasn't even sure what "corporate law stuff" was; I just knew I didn't really want to work for a law firm, big or small.

"How do you know if you haven't even tried it?" she said.

"True," I said, thinking about making some real money, just for one summer, which could help pay off some of my student loans. "Okay," I said, resigned, and perhaps a teeny bit excited (not that I would have admitted it). "Sign me up. What do I have to do for the writing test?"

I entered the program, submitted my résumé and writing test—and lo and behold, I was asked to interview with three big law firms in New York. After a bit of should-I-or-shouldn't-I grief, and persuading myself that it was just for *one* summer, I decided to go for it. I accepted a job as a first-year summer associate with Chadbourne & Parke. It was thrilling and a little embarrassing at the same time. Me—working at a law firm! In New York! I could hardly believe it, particularly when I found out how much I'd be paid: a little over $1,000 per week. I was proud but also felt like a bit of a sellout. Most of my law school friends were having a hard time even finding a job after their first year, and were jealous of those of us who had paying jobs, much less a gig with a prestigious New York law firm.

I managed to get over my guilt pretty easily. I was also excited to return to New York for the summer—although I wouldn't be returning to Doug. The distance and my hectic studying schedule had proved too much for our relationship to handle, and I'd broken up with him early into spring semester. At the time, I thought he was done with law school for good; I had no idea that just a few months later, I'd be starting my second year of law school at UT, and he'd be starting his first.

That summer, I quickly discovered that I was the only first-year summer associate at Chadbourne, and as if that wasn't enough to make me feel out of place, I also discovered that I was also completely unprepared to work in an office environment. I had gone from dance classes to bartending (and dancing on bars) to modeling (which was sometimes more of the same), and then after a year of law school, had landed a job that found me assigned to a beautiful, dark-wood-furnished office, a legal team—and a secretary. It was a whole new world. I'd never had a secretary, and I really didn't know what to do with one. She was constantly asking, "What can I do for you?" I was uncomfortable with the concept of having someone else do my menial tasks or grunt work; it's just not how I was raised. Finally, one day while I was making copies (not realizing the other summer associates weren't making their own copies), I found myself being confronted.

"Ms. Huskey!" my secretary said. "No, no, no! Let me do that for you. You can't be making copies!"

I was mortified, partly because I was perfectly capable of making my own copies, and partly because I was completely unprepared for a confrontation with an underutilized secretary. I realized that she was there to help me be more efficient, and vowed to be better at delegating, but even after I got a little more comfortable doing so, it was always, "Do you think you would mind doing this for me, if you have the time, please?" Most of my coworkers, on the other hand, looked like they had been born to wear a suit and sit in a fancy office, ordering their assistants around.

During the summer, the law firms woo you, which basically means one thing: summer associate outings. There were dinners, drinks, Yankees games, long lunches at the best restaurants in town, concerts—you name it. Law firms put your entire summer social calendar all together in one nice package.

Most large firms have a "summer program committee" devoted to making sure summer associates have a good time during their time at the firm. I thought this was all wonderful, especially the long lunches at places like Aquavit, La Cote Basque, Le Colonial, Judson Grill, Smith & Wollensky, and Il Nido.

Last but not least, there's the actual legal work a summer associate does at a law firm, though it seems that the summer program is less about the work and more about meeting the people at the firm. Truthfully, most big law firms do roughly the same thing, have similar clients, and make you work similarly hard, so what really matters is whether you fit in with the "firm culture"—the personalities of the other attorneys—and whether you can imagine working until midnight, night after night, with these people. At Chadbourne, I worked in the litigation practice group, primarily getting exposure to a few different cases. I did a lot of research and writing of legal memorandums, under the supervision of a litigation partner, Gary Morrisroe, a savvy litigator who was very patient with me and my dearth of experience. I also spent a lot of time in a storage closet filled with boxes and boxes of depositions from the DeLorean case (the wealthy automobile family), looking for a particular answer by a witness whose name couldn't quite be recalled, hence the needle-in-the-haystack assignment. That was the unattractive, though hardly rare, side of big law firm work.

Working at my first law firm was an eye-opening experience in a lot of ways—and not just because I was tasked with getting used to having a secretary. I was taking it all in: the paychecks, the long lunches at fancy restaurants, the suits, the handshakes (even shaking the hand of everyone you met was new to me; I was used to raising my shot glass and shouting "Cheers!"), the really nice offices. . . . It was tantalizing, like a shimmering mirage in the middle of the desert. (And I would know.) What made it so appealing, to me, was that it was so well run. The entire operation was so organized, so together; I really liked that. It was efficient and productive in ways that a girl who had grown up with an ex-military hunter-fisherman father could appreciate. And not only that—the work was challenging in ways that even my first year of law school had not been. It was extremely cerebral and incredibly complex, and I found that really exciting. Furthermore, the intensity with which each lawyer worked every day (New York lawyers in particular are very intense) impressed me. Lawyers in law firms seemed so well-spoken, smart, savvy, and worldly. They were problem solvers; they were "doers." I found that very appealing. I wanted to be a doer, too, and work in this kind of legal world.

The fall semester of second year is a mess at almost every law school in the nation—it's high season for recruiting 2Ls to work the following summer, and potentially permanently (after graduation and passing the bar). In the fall, UT Law holds on-campus interviews, or "OCIs," where numerous employers—mainly law firms, but also some government agencies—come to campus and conduct thirty-minute interviews all day long.

Students submit their résumés in advance, hoping to get selected for an interview, where one or two lawyers from the firm will size you up, make sure you don't drool, and ask you obvious questions, such as "What do you like about civil procedure?" or not-so-obvious questions, like "Where do you go for your favorite margarita?" (I was actually asked this question by two smart, very cool, female litigators from Sheppard Mullin, a big law firm in Los Angeles; their laid-back, non-lawyerlike question made me extra interested in their firm.)

If you don't drool, answer appropriately, and manage to stand out from the fifteen or twenty other law students they interviewed, you get a "callback," where you are flown to the headquarters of the firm for more interviews and a fancy lunch. If they really like you, they may also take you out to dinner. The final goal of this whole process is to secure a summer associate position during the summer between your second and third years of law school. Ideally, after your stint as a summer associate, you are offered a permanent job at the firm, which usually happens as long as you haven't totally screwed things up during the summer. This takes place before you've even started your third year, and it's referred to as an "offer." (All this interviewing and performing felt a little like modeling all over again, with the callbacks and offers.) This means a large number of law students have accepted their post–law school, post–bar passage jobs *by their third year of law school.*

As a second-year law student, I was distracted from my fall classes by doing a ton of interviewing for a second-year summer associate position. I was a commodity because I was female, in the top 25 percent of my class, and part Asian—practically the poster child for diversity. I spent so much time interviewing with firms in New York that I missed a lot of classes and had to rely on friends' notes. I was lucky to take Evidence with Megan, who also had a lot of callbacks out of town, and we both managed to do quite well in Professor Goode's class through our system of tape-recording lectures and sharing notes. It was a really busy time of interviews, classes, and studying—and then there was Doug.

Doug had managed to get a full scholarship to UT even though he'd deferred his enrollment for a year. As a 1L, he was busy with classes and studying, but I quickly realized he wasn't too busy to chase after me. I'd always had a hard time saying no to him, and soon after he arrived for orientation, we decided to try to work things out. Eventually, it didn't, and we broke up. (Again.) On this go-around we had a hard time even remaining friends, so I thought our on-again, off-again status had finally been set in the "off" position.

The school year went by quickly, and before I knew it, April had arrived, with my summer associate position just around the corner. I had hardly talked to Doug all year, and then suddenly, seemingly out of the blue, we found ourselves speaking—and quickly dating again. *How had this happened?* I was a planner, always prepared, but I had not planned on dating Doug again. I tried not to overthink it; I was just happy we were back together. Though I wouldn't have admitted it, I had missed his

New York personality, his edginess, and his sharp wit. Within a couple of weeks, not one to move cautiously, Doug proposed. It was completely unexpected, but when he asked me to marry him, the word *Yes!* came flying out of my mouth. I felt like it was the right decision, even if it hadn't been very well thought out. I loved him, after all.

My hard work and interviewing in my second year had led me to accept a summer associate position with Shearman & Sterling LLP, for the summer in between my second and third years of law school. I was intrigued by the international nature of the firm—it had offices all over the world—and I liked the fact that if I ended up with a permanent job with them, I could put in a request to work in one of their international offices for a few years. My summer had been decided: Doug and I would return to New York, I would work for Shearman, and he would look for a job.

It was hard to get a job as a first-year; I knew that I'd been lucky to find an opportunity through UT's Career Services Office. But Doug's first-year grades weren't stellar, and he had a hard time getting interviews, let alone an offer to join a firm as a summer associate (or any legal job, for that matter). It didn't make much of a difference, though, because we both still planned to return to New York. What made my summer associate experience with Shearman different, though, was that I got to spend half of the summer in the New York office—the firm's headquarters, with about six hundred attorneys—and the other half in one of its branch offices. Shearman's summer program form, which I had to fill out well in advance, allowed you to choose two different practice groups and split your summer between two different offices. Not being one to turn down travel, I put an X in the box marked "Paris."

"Ms. Huskey, this is the summer program coordinator in the New York office of Shearman & Sterling," a brusque voice said over the phone.

"Yes?" I answered, immediately worried. *Oh jeez, did I fill out the form wrong? Did they catch on to the fact that I'm not really supposed to be working in a big fancy New York law firm?* I assumed the worst—they were about to revoke my summer position.

"I see you put down that you'd like to split your summer with the Paris office," the voice said. "Do you speak French?"

"Umm . . ." I stalled for time, tempted to say yes but thinking that my high school French, while it had gotten me through on more than one occasion in Angola, was probably not going to go over as well in a law office where you have ethical obligations to your clients. I started imagining how I would be disbarred before I even got started. "Not really," I confessed.

"Well, how about one of our other offices? Hong Kong? Washington, D.C.?" the coordinator asked.

Hong Kong sounded fun, but it was far away. "Really? I can spend half of my summer in D.C., just like that?" I was a little baffled that such things could be so easily arranged, but also starting to get a little more insight into Shearman's world, where thousands and thousands of dollars are spent on its summer program just to keep its summer associates happy. My somewhat whimsical decision landed me in Washington, D.C., an experience that would ultimately decide my future.

Though Shearman's summer program turned out to be twice as big and twice as generous as Chadbourne's had been, my experiences in Shearman's New York office were similar to what I'd experienced during my summer at Chadbourne— except that instead of trying out litigation, which I had enjoyed, I'd decided to try out something different. I chose to test out a stint in corporate law—international corporate law, to be precise. It was a bloody disaster! Despite the word "international," it was the most boring work I could possibly imagine. It ended up being a lot of cut-and-paste, faxing contracts back and forth for approval, and being asked to change one word here and another word there, right up until one o'clock in the morning. I hated it. Corporate law was not for me, and I realized it right away. I was also starting to think the New York office wasn't for me, either. Thankfully, I had chosen to work in the litigation practice group the second half of the summer, in D.C.

Washington was a breath of fresh air. The office was smaller (with only twenty attorneys), and therefore less hierarchical. I got to work directly with the partners, and the people (both the attorneys and the administrative staff) in the D.C. office were somewhat anti-authoritarian; they resented the New York office for looking down at them as if they were the baby brother in the family. The D.C. Shearman attorneys were much more laid-back than their stiff-necked New York colleagues. They invited the administrative staff to join them on firm outings, they played in a softball league, they talked about their kids or the new hobby they had picked up. They had *lives*. Beyond the courtroom, I mean. Working in D.C. gave me an entirely different outlook on what life as a lawyer could be like.

You could actually have a life if you worked here, I thought. New York had been fun, with all the fancy summer lunches, but everyone had *really* been into working hard. I'd never been opposed to hard work; it was required in my family. But in New York, it was a badge of honor to stay later than your office neighbor, and you were definitely a "star associate" if you worked through the weekend. Ugh! Why the New York attorneys looked down on their D.C. counterparts, who worked less and made the same salary, I'll never know. And, the D.C. area had a cheaper cost of living. There were big sidewalks and short buildings. It wasn't the concrete jungle that New York was. I felt like in D.C. I could be a real person, someone more well-rounded than the typical intense, overworked New York attorney. The atmosphere in the D.C. office showed me a particular lifestyle I could maintain as an attorney, and that was the kind of life I wanted—at least in the short term. *I can talk Doug into living here*, I thought. *What's not to like?*

Apparently, a lot. But Doug and I couldn't agree on what those things were, exactly. As I had hoped, I received an offer from Shearman to work there permanently after my third year, and I was thrilled. I couldn't wait to get back to D.C. and begin my law career at a place as prestigious as Shearman & Sterling.

I knew I was making the right choice. *Wasn't I?* I pondered this only briefly. There was no shortage of law firms with unhappy lawyers. They don't like what they do, they don't like the firm they work late into the night for, but they're stuck—or so they say—stuck with student loans or mortgages and an obligation to work in a field they had chosen and worked so hard to join.

The attrition rate at any major law firm is about four years on average. Most lawyers only last that long before moving on to something less demanding because they just burn out. It's hard to manage the constant intensity, the hours, the expectations. You basically have no freedom. Partners can cancel your vacation at the very last minute because of a breakthrough (or lack thereof) in a case or a deal. Your family becomes a group of strangers because of the long hours you put in at the office. It can be really brutal, and I'd seen the ugly side of it in New York (and in the lawyer we had met during our backpacking travels). Yet, as you go through law school, you begin to see your future taking shape. Often, once you've started, you feel as if you have set yourself on a certain path that you can't step off of.

The change in me came slowly, but I noticed it. I wondered what had happened to the combat boots–wearing punkster from New York who wanted more than anything to change the world by doing public interest work. Where did she go? Honestly, I don't know. She sort of disappeared, or at least went underground and into hiding for the time being. Working for Shearman in D.C. had given me hope that I could like my job and the career I had just spent three years and thousands of

dollars training for; that I could have a good and—let's face it—
very comfortable life, one where I might get to see my husband
once in a while; that I didn't have to automatically give up all
of the things I'd come to enjoy simply because I was a lawyer.
If I chose to work in Shearman's New York office, on the other
hand, I foresaw a life of misery and despair . . . and endless billable hours.

Doug, however, was not convinced. He thought we should
go to New York (his friends were still there and still a big draw
for him), and, therefore, I should go to Shearman's New York
office. I had accepted Shearman's offer, but could defer starting for another year—and therefore defer the choice between
New York and D.C., too. Since Doug had another year of law
school left, I scrambled to find a job to keep me in Austin
another year, and was able to get a local judicial clerkship. I
could start at Shearman after I clerked. In general, law firms
will hold your job for you for a year so that you can gain the
kind of prestigious experience that is only earned by working
as a clerk for a judge. Many law firms will pay you a clerkship
bonus when you eventually do start (for making the financial
sacrifice of working for the government), *and* you don't have
to lose a year. You start at the firm as a second-year associate,
on second-year salary. By accepting a position with a judge in
Austin, I could stay with Doug while he completed his third
year of law school. I figured the year of clerking would just
give me more time to convince Doug that moving to D.C. was
the right thing to do.

After graduating from law school, I spent the summer studying for the bar exam and working a few weeks in Shearman's D.C. office. Doug was unable to get a summer associate position or any paying job during his second-year summer, and since we were planning on a wedding at the end of summer, at least one of us had to work to pay for it all. It was a small affair, and despite what would eventually happen between us, the wedding turned out to be very easygoing and a lot of fun.

We enjoyed a brief honeymoon in Costa Rica, returning to Austin so that Doug could start his third year, and I could begin my clerkship at the Third Court of Appeals in Austin, a state appellate court. Working as a judicial clerk turned out to be beneficial in a lot of ways I couldn't have predicted. First, it's a guaranteed "in" if you later find yourself in front of that court or in front of the judge you once clerked for; second, it provides you with direct insight into how courts work, and, in particular, how judges tend to look at everything about a case, from the behavior by attorneys to the briefs they submit. Since I had decided to pursue litigation, not corporate law, I would presumably be spending a lot of my time in court and before judges, and this kind of insider knowledge would really pay off.

My clerkship was with Justice Bea Ann Smith, who became my mentor and friend during our year together, and would remain so over the years as I practiced and then later taught law. The judge-clerk relationship is such an intimate one; judges and clerks will either form very close relationships—or really terrible ones. Luckily for me, clerking for Justice Smith was a wonderful experience . . . mostly.

Judge Smith is truly an original. On the Texas appellate court, in Austin, there were six sitting judges, and each had a clerk. We clerks were all in the same boat: fresh out of law school, most of us with some plan or another on what we would be doing after our year of clerking. I knew I was in for quite an experience when, on the first day, one of the other clerks found out I was clerking for Judge Smith.

She leaned over to whisper in my ear: "Ooh, Kristine . . . you're working for the toughest judge on the court."

"Really?" I asked. *Oh no*, I thought. *What have I gotten myself into?*

"Judge Smith *is* tough," my fellow clerk answered, sensing my anxiety. "But she's fair."

I wasn't really comforted by her answer. In truth, my colleague was right. Judge Smith is tough. She's tough on the lawyers who stand before her, forcing them to state and stand behind their positions and articulate why she should go their way. She's also tough on her fellow judges, making them explain in detail the rationale behind their opinions, especially when they disagree with her. She's tough on her clerks, too, and it's a good thing she is. Basically, it's a clerk's job to prepare the judge for the cases they will be hearing in oral argument. If your judge ends up writing the opinion on the case, you have to draft the opinion for them. You turn it in to your judge and receive it back a few days later with spurts of red ink all over it—editing marks everywhere. Sometimes I would dread going into Judge Smith's chambers because I knew she would have plenty to say about the work I'd done. It was good for me, I kept telling myself, but that didn't make listening to her "constructive criticism" or answering to her intense questioning any easier.

On the other hand, Judge Smith is one of the nicest, most gracious, most interesting women I've ever met. She has been a role model for me ever since I clerked for her in 1997. She's one of those women you have to admire for her tenacity, energy, and positive approach to life. It's very difficult to become a judge in Texas, and she went to UT Law School at a time when it wasn't all that common to be a female lawyer. And yet, she did it all—she graduated with honors, worked full-time for a law firm, became an adjunct professor, got married, had kids, and somehow got on track to become a judge. She was a very focused attorney and judge, and never, not once in her life, has she ever been intellectually lazy, even though many judges can be, and are.

Now retired, Judge Smith remains curious and intensely passionate about so many things in life outside of the law. She loves the arts, loves to travel (a girl after my own heart), and enjoys the outdoors, particularly when she's got a fishing rod in her hands. She's a true Renaissance woman, and working for her only deepened my resolve to choose the D.C. office over the New York office when it came time for me to make a decision about which Shearman office I would request.

It didn't help our situation that Doug still hadn't managed to get a job during his last year at law school. By the time I had to fill out the paperwork to join Shearman permanently and request an office location, I was ready to stand my ground.

"All of our friends are in New York," he said. It was the standard response, and I was tired of it.

"Doug," I sighed, "if we move to New York and I work in the New York office, you will never see me. I will work around the clock, and I will be miserable. What kind of marriage will we have?"

"But *I'll* be so much happier in New York," he responded. "I don't know anybody in D.C. My friends are in New York, and if I don't have a job, I'll be depressed. It will be helpful to have my friends around."

You and your friends, I thought. I was frustrated with his logic. It was as if he were saying, "I plan on being a failure, so I might as well set myself up for being a comfortable one." I couldn't believe that once again he seemed to be choosing his friends over me, but this time, I wasn't going to let him get away with it.

"Look, Doug—I'm the one with a job," I said. "D.C. will be better for both of us. We'll have a life, and it's not like there aren't legal jobs there. You'll find a good one pretty easily. Washington is the better choice for us, as a couple."

How could he argue? Judge Smith had taught me well. I was becoming more of a lawyer every day.

8

Two Toms and a Jobie

By the time we arrived in Washington, D.C., in the fall of 1998, I was itching to get started on my shiny new law career; I wanted to start *practicing* law, not just write draft opinions. I'd finished up my clerkship, Doug had graduated, and life was good. Although I'd missed out on my actual first year with Shearman, I had discovered it was probably a blessing in disguise. I'd heard horror stories from friends of first-year all-nighters, and "document review," where poor, new associates are tasked with wading through boxes and boxes of documents, thousands and thousands of pages of reading, summarizing, organizing, and compiling, all in hopes of finding those thirty or so documents that will either make your case or break your opponent's case. My clerkship had allowed me second-year status; I entered the firm as if I had already worked there for a year, with the salary to prove it.

I stared at my first paycheck in disbelief. My mom and I giggled together over the phone about it when she told me she made about half that and she had been a nurse for almost thirty years. *How did I get here?* I marveled. I had lived through it— four years working my way through Columbia, another three years at UT Law—and yet, it took a while for the reality to truly sink in.

I am a lawyer, I thought. And then, *Correction: An attorney*. Most lawyers refer to themselves as attorneys, not lawyers (maybe because there are plenty of lawyer jokes, but not too many attorney jokes). *A real, live attorney, in a top law firm in Washington, D.C., with my own office, my own secretary, and a closet full of office supplies.*

I had earned the job, sure, but for the first few weeks, it was all completely surreal. Shearman's offices were on Pennsylvania Avenue in the heart of D.C., with views of the National Archives, The Mall, and the Navy Memorial. It was so grown-up. *No more dancing on bars for you, Huskey*. I gave myself a silent pep talk. *This is the big time. You wear a suit to work. You are a professional.*

Any attorney will tell you that your first year in a law firm can be unbelievably overwhelming. Everybody, from the associates and partners to the administrative staff, including the copy-room workers—they all know you're new. Though you technically rank higher than the individuals who make you copies or fix your computer, you know much less than they do about how the firm operates, so it pays to listen well, take notes, and be nice. (Besides, being an overbearing attorney with the administrative staff is truly obnoxious.) Moreover, the firm isn't as interested in pampering you, now that you're officially a member of the firm and not a summer associate they are trying to woo. The honeymoon is over. The attorneys in the office know you don't have a heavy caseload (yet). They know you're just starting to sort out the relationships between the associates and the partners; who works well together, who's working on which cases, which cases are the ones to get in on and which ones you should stay away from at all cost. And, like it or not, you are fresh meat. The sharks don't waste any time—they begin to circle immediately.

"Kristine, right?" One of my new colleagues was standing at the doorway to my office. "Welcome to Shearman."

"Thank you!" I said, immediately suspicious. *What's with the welcome wagon? Are people really that nice here?*

"How are things so far?" he asked.

"Good, good. I'm really looking forward to getting to know everyone." *What does he mean by "How are things?" Like, did I have a nice lunch? Or do I have work to do yet? Maybe he wants to know whether I received my Westlaw pass code so I can start researching cases right away.* Westlaw and LexisNexis have a monopoly on electronic legal databases, but I'd always been a Westlaw gal myself.

"Great," responded my be-suited colleague. I couldn't remember his name, and certainly didn't want to ask, in case he was a partner or someone else I should *definitely* know immediately. "Do you have a few minutes? Can I sit down?" he asked, sliding into one of my fancy new chairs without waiting for an answer. *Oh no, here it comes, another pitch.* Just as I suspected, the mid-level associate (I was sure by now he wasn't a partner or a senior associate) launched into the presentation of a case that I could tell was being embellished somewhat for my benefit. "Let me know if you're interested, okay? I'm just down the hall," he said, finishing his performance.

I'd had the same conversation—about various cases the firm was handling—a few times already that week. I didn't have fifteen minutes to myself, to get organized, before the next person would stop by, sometimes just to say hello and sometimes with a pitch. It was true; I didn't have anything big on my plate just yet, aside from a couple of memorandums to research and write, and recovering from watching the employee training video on insider trading (they really try to scare the crap out of you by citing the numbers of young attorneys who go to jail each year for engaging in these corporate misdeeds). But I hardly knew which work I should be taking on, or which teams I hoped to work with yet.

As I had requested, I was assigned to the "international litigation and arbitration group," which meant that most of my work would be on cases that were in some stage of litigation, and that I would work with partners and other associates who were also in litigation. I also requested the opportunity to try out some "international trade" work, which involves representing foreign companies that have been accused of "dumping," or selling their commodity on the U.S. market below market price.

When I was a summer associate at Shearman, I had worked primarily with Steve Marzen, an incredibly smart junior partner who had gone to Harvard and clerked for Justice Stevens on the U.S. Supreme Court. He could be very intense, and his enthusiasm for mentoring young lawyers was about as extreme as his carrot-topped head; he was one of the main reasons I'd accepted a permanent position at Shearman. Naturally, I did some work with him when I first arrived. We represented a company out of Italy that made the bone screws used to immobilize broken bones so that they would heal properly. Steve delighted in describing to me (in detail) how these devices worked. I was very squeamish about medical devices and tried hard to keep my happy face in position while Steve went on about the novel design and what it did to the body. He was exactly right: Their design was so novel and so good that it had been stolen by another company, whom we promptly sued. I was happy to get my start as a lawyer doing some actual work on a case.

I chose to work in the D.C. office of Shearman & Sterling because it was a small operation; it didn't have enough manpower to allow associates to spend hours and hours on document review. I got to be involved in many aspects of the cases I worked on, whereas in most big law offices, the "junior associates" (lawyers at a law firm who are one to three years out of law school) can end up doing document review—and only document review—for an entire year, sometimes more. We'd all heard the urban legend of a Skadden & Arps associate who did nothing but document review for two years. Luckily for me, during my entire eight-year tenure at Shearman, I had to do very little "time" in document-review prison—a couple of days in New York, a few days in London, and then later on, running my own review in Bermuda. (Oh, that was tough all right!) If you're going to do document review, you might as well do it someplace interesting.

In the beginning, for me, it was a lot of research and memorandum-writing. A partner would cruise by my office and ask, "Hi! Are you busy? Could you write a memo on this very discrete issue for me?" The answer was always yes. And the issue was never discrete. Instead of the "short time" it took to research the issue, as the partner had suggested, it took long hours, sometimes even days or weeks, because the law in question was about as clear as mud. I eventually learned that a "discrete" issue was code for "I have no idea what the law is or how long you will have to spend finding the answer to my question." I did a lot of what we liked to call "scorch the Earth" research, sorting through hundreds of cases looking for any that might have a bearing on a particular issue among numerous others in the case we were working on.

"In response to your question," I would write for the partners after hours of research, "the short answer is: It's highly probable, though certainly not guaranteed, that [client X] will lose on the issue of whether [client X]'s contacts with the relevant jurisdiction were either substantial or continuous and systematic enough for the court to find personal jurisdiction over [client X]. Pursuant to [*Whoosywhatsit v. Whatchamacallit*], the court will likely view [client X]'s bank account and previously owned franchise, both though now defunct, in the relevant jurisdiction as constituting sufficient minimum contacts and satisfying the due process test set out in the seminal *Worldwide Volkswagen* and *Asahi* cases." The "short" answer would always be followed by the much longer answer, setting out in detail the support—citing case law, statutes, and any other relevant law—for the short answer.

I spent an astounding amount of time doing research to find an answer to what started out as just one question, but would quickly balloon into several trails that needed to be followed. At $125 per hour for billing, the totals added up quickly. It was a complete novelty to me, a girl who had paid her way through Columbia by booking as many go-sees and serving as many drinks as she could, that I could do something as simple as reading and summarizing a case and bill more for a day's work than I ever could have made as a model. *How can companies afford these legal fees?* I used to wonder. It was just the beginning, for me, of learning just how much money big corporations made in net profits alone and how willing they were to spend hundreds of thousands of dollars in legal fees to defend or pursue a case.

Eventually, I began working regularly with one partner in particular, Tom Martin. Tom was the managing partner of the D.C. office, and when he asked you to do something, not only did you do it—you made it your top priority. Tom was the kind of colleague I was drawn to: He was tall and imposing, intellectual and very wise, an intimidating character to most. I found him to be a kindred spirit once I got to know him because on the inside, he was a little wacky and liked to go against the tide.

In the beginning, however, I simply respected and feared him, like most of the other junior associates.

Tom had asked me to research a teeny piece of one of his current litigation cases. Our firm was representing three individuals (technically, "liquidators") who were in charge of liquidating a company that had been headquartered in Bermuda. It was a complex case involving the Electric Mutual Liability Insurance Company (EMLICO), the company that had insured General Electric (GE) for a majority of its liabilities. EMLICO had run into trouble when GE began getting sued for asbestos and environmental problems; they just didn't have the cash available to cover the insurance it had sold. When EMLICO tried to recover some insurance money of its own to cover what it needed to pay out (from a "reinsurer," a company that insures an insurance company), its claim was denied.

Enter Shearman & Sterling and Tom Martin—and a bit later, me. For the next four years this case would consume me. It would see me struggling through a difficult personal life, including an eventual divorce; coming into my own as a lawyer; and, finally, learning what it meant to be me. Although I was a professional attorney with serious responsibilities, I was still the combat boots–clad girl who talked back to her professors.

When I first started on the case, I was researching "discrete" reinsurance issues (and the industry itself) and writing short memorandums. By the end of the case, four years later, I was giving closing arguments in an arbitration that had seen over seventy-five days of trial and fifteen witnesses, and had forty-five million dollars at stake. In a sense, I cut my lawyer teeth on that case, growing up as an attorney as we marched through the various stages of an arbitration that ultimately ended with a judgment in favor of our client (if I might say so myself).

At the start of the EMLICO case, I worked primarily with Tom Martin; Jobie Shally, a counsel who worked in the New York office; and Roland Schroeder, a senior associate at the time in the D.C. office.

The litigation practice in D.C. was mostly male, with no female partners and very few female senior associates, and almost as soon as I met her, Jobie became another role model for me. She was simply stunning in all respects—incredibly smart and strategic. Further, Jobie is a beautiful woman, and she never tried to hide it, unlike most female lawyers I'd met. Female attorneys in D.C. were generally frumpy, conservative in both dress and mannerisms. Jobie was the complete opposite. She wore ultra-fashionable suits with miniskirts and skyscraper-high heels at the end of long skinny legs. Her hair was wild and curly, and she almost never wore it pulled back. For such a slender gal, she was surprisingly loud (still is), but she was feminine and smart, and never shy about speaking up when she had an opinion. She seemed to be able to balance her work life with her personal life, working incredibly long hours on the case but still making time for her family and herself, and, more significantly, not being afraid to talk about the importance of family time, downtime, and fun time. She was everything I wanted to be.

Although she worked as hard as any junior associate, Jobie reminded me not to take work too seriously—that there was more to life than billable hours. "Kristine, why are you worried about going on vacation? That's why we have big teams, so we can cover for each other. C'mon, you think we are actually going to miss you? This is Shearman, remember? Everyone is dispensable."

Jobie also taught me that playing with the big boys didn't mean no play at all. One time at a dinner meeting with Chris, our liquidator (headquartered at PricewaterhouseCoopers in London), we'd just polished off our third three-hundred-dollar bottle of wine. Suddenly Jobie leaned forward in her chair and started doing some sort of odd dance move with just her shoulders.

"What are you doing?" the client asked Jobie. Completely serious, Jobie's hand rose from beneath the table. Crumpled in her fist were her stockings, which she had managed to slip off while we were talking about our witnesses! "I hate these things!" Jobie said, stuffing them in her empty wineglass without interrupting the flow of the conversation. Jobie was about a hundred and five pounds dripping wet, but she was larger than life.

Needless to say, after getting a taste of what it was like to work with Tom and Jobie, I was thrilled when my name finally made it onto the EMLICO "players list" (a list of who's who on a case—attorneys, client representatives, consultants, etc.). I realized I was now considered an official part of the EMLICO team (and not just an associate who wrote random memos on reinsurance). I got to work alongside hot-shot Jobie *and* the D.C. office's managing partner, whose reputation for top-notch lawyering extended well beyond our firm, and I got in on the ground floor, when the arbitration had just begun.

It kept me busy; in those years, I billed twenty-four hundred to twenty-five hundred hours a year. To keep that in perspective, working that many *billable* hours (not including time spent organizing arbitrary documents on my desk and floor, of which there were always numerous piles, performing administrative tasks, interviewing potential summer associates, or going on summer associate lunches) means that I billed about three hundred hours a month—about seventy-five hours per week, sometimes more, with no time off. If you took a vacation, it meant that when you returned, you had to work more than seventy-five hours a week just to make up for the days that you didn't bill any time. There were weeks when I worked until ten or eleven p.m., night after night after night. And on top of that, one year I took on about five hundred hours of *pro bono* work. Mind you, I was not unique; many attorneys at big firms work at least that much, or up to three thousand billable hours a year. Just the thought of working that many hours on big law firm type cases makes me sweat.

Of course, there were several reasons for my heavy workload. One was that the case I was working on *was* truly demanding. Another was that I really enjoyed the work. A third reason was because I simply dreaded going home. When it finally hit me how hard I'd been working, it was a genuine surprise. *Wow,*

I thought, *it's been six months since I've had a full weekend off.*
I was far from the exception; the attrition rate at big law firms
is so high because it's hard to sustain that kind of workload,
whether it's for a short time or indefinitely. It's easy to see why
lawyers have high incidences of drug and alcohol abuse, and—
as I was about to discover—a high divorce rate. We work hard,
we play hard. And we are, in many ways, "married" to our
jobs.

Most litigators end up juggling several cases at once; while
one case is just beginning its discovery phase, another is waiting for the court to rule on a pending motion to dismiss, and
you may have one or two others that are in various phases of
litigation as well. During the downtime in the EMLICO case,
I started working with another Tom from Shearman—Tom
Wilner, a senior litigation and international trade partner.
International trade, while it sounds really cool, often involves a
company's operating costs and profits, and requires an understanding of the economics of the market system. Many summer
associates yelp with glee when assigned to work on an "international trade" case, only to run screaming later on when they
find out that it involves lots of numbers, and not WTO (World
Trade Organization) policy or law as they'd hoped.

Tom was leading the charge on a case in which our firm represented the Organization of Petroleum Exporting Companies
(OPEC), which was being sued for antitrust violations, a type
of law that exists to prohibit monopolies from dominating the
market. Imagine that—OPEC getting sued for being a cartel!

At first, Tom asked me to look up a few cases and summarize them for use in a brief he was writing. He liked the job I did, so he asked me to draft a small section of the brief that addressed personal jurisdiction, my favorite topic from law school (Professor Issacharoff would have been proud). Tom was pleased with my work, and just as pleased with my attitude. I was never deferential to any of the D.C. partners in my firm (in New York, I mostly just tried to stay away from the partners). I spoke up when I had something to say, and working with Jobie made me realize I didn't have to rein in my personality quite as much as I'd thought—and it showed.

"I just don't understand it," Tom W. said to me, shaking his head with mock disapproval. "All of the other associates are so deferential, and you're not. Why is that?"

"Tom," I began, matching his playful tone, "I'm the girl who talks back. I don't take shit from people. And besides, you like that I treat you as if I'm your equal, don't you?"

He feigned shock. "But I'm a senior partner, Kristine!"

"And you'd hate to be patronized," I shot back with a smile.

I'm not sure whether it was my work or my attitude that first caught Tom's attention at the firm, but we worked well together and were destined to become not only a great working team but also great "buddies," as he affectionately referred to me down the road. Neither of us had any idea that a few years later we would take on a case that would put us, and our firm, in the national and international spotlight. We simply enjoyed working together, which was how I ended up traveling to Vienna, where OPEC is headquartered, for a meeting with the infamous OPEC oil ministers. I soon found out it wasn't just a meeting with the oil ministers; we were actually joining in on their notorious biannual meeting, where the ministers discuss oil prices and often make the decision to pump more or less oil for world consumption.

When we got to OPEC's offices, I was shocked to find hordes of press, with ropes keeping them from rushing at us. Cameras were flashing, microphones were being shoved at our faces; it was the kind of fame I'd dreamed of years earlier, when I'd hoped to become a famous face, but not the kind of fame I'd anticipated when I'd decided to become an attorney.

We were ushered into the inner sanctum of OPEC's headquarters, where only the top officials and their attorneys—us— were allowed to go. The president of OPEC, Dr. Chakib Khelil from Algeria, introduced us: "Oil ministers of OPEC, please meet your attorneys, Tom Wilner and Kristine Huskey." In that moment, I experienced the first of what I call "Dear Mom" moments; an event so unbelievable that I thought it would be something my mom would want me to write home about. When the president said my name out loud, I began composing a letter to my mother in my head: *Dear Mom*, it would begin. *You will not believe what just happened to me. I have just been introduced to the oil ministers of OPEC . . . as their attorney.*

After our introduction, we were asked to sit in some empty chairs behind one intimidating character, the oil minister from

Libya, with his trademark turban and wildly unkempt beard. Tom was having similar thoughts, although I doubted he was composing a letter to his own mother. "Imagine this, Kristine," he said. "Here we are, Americans, sitting next to the oil minister of Libya, as his lawyers. Libya, the great foe of the United States."

Tom and I next worked together representing the Mexican tomato industry—the *entire* Mexican tomato industry. The client representatives we worked with were essentially the country's tomato farmers, who were on the verge of being sued for "anti-dumping," which meant they were about to be accused of infringing on domestic (American) tomato farmers' business by driving prices down and selling their own Mexican tomatoes more cheaply than American tomatoes ("dumping" their goods on the market). If you think America is all about capitalism and the free market; think again. There are laws, both domestic and international, that regulate the sale of goods by foreign companies on the domestic market. American companies are very vigilant about tracking the prices of everything, from tomatoes to pasta to rubber tires.

For me, the case revealed a whole new side of being an attorney: Finally, I didn't have to draft memos or do inordinate amounts of legal research. Instead, I was able to use the experience I'd gained over the past few years to work toward negotiating an agreement between the U.S. Department of Commerce (DOC) and the Mexican tomato industry that would satisfy all interested parties—the DOC, the American and the Mexican tomato farmers, and the Mexican government, who, of course, had a huge interest in the health of a large national industry. Tom and I spent a lot of time traveling to Mexico City to meet with our clients and representatives from the Mexican government. So far, in almost every case I'd worked on at Shearman, I'd been surrounded by men. The only female I had gotten to work with was Jobie, and even then, our clients in the EMLICO case were male, our witnesses were mostly male, and our Shearman teammates (the lawyers) were male. The Mexican tomato farmers' case was no exception. I spent many a lunch with Tom, Jeronimo Gomez del Campo, who was a male associate on the case, and ten to twelve of our clients, all men, eating steak, sipping tequila, and discussing tomato-growing costs and the inclement weather that had affected past crops.

Working on the tomato case was when I really got to know (and trust) Tom Wilner, and vice versa. At first, the tomato farmers didn't know what to make of me, a young, attractive, female lawyer, who was treated like an equal by a senior partner who had thirty-five years of lawyering experience. Tom unflinchingly gave me credit for all of my ideas in front of the clients, the Mexican and U.S. government reps, and opposing counsel. This sort of acknowledgment is extremely rare in big law firms. Tom worked hard to build up my confidence and to engender a sense of trust in me by others, including our clients. This can be a difficult thing to do in a law firm because of the rigid hierarchy; there are so many people above each member of the firm.

This provided an environment in which I could be a smart, kick-ass attorney, but still be me. Tom, Jeronimo, and the clients treated me like "one of the boys" while still recognizing that I was, in fact, the only female in a sea of men, alternatively teasing me and treating me like a rose among thorns. One night after a long steak dinner in Washington with the tomato farmers, we decided to let loose a little and go out for drinks in Georgetown. We ended up at the Guards, a pub and restaurant, and after a few rounds, I whipped out the draft agreement, suggesting an idea that had been whirling around in my head all through dinner. Martin Ley, one of the tomato farmers, immediately saw the significance of my idea, which we discussed until the manager told us it was time to pack it in. Later, Martin would remind everyone that I came up with the great idea over midnight cocktails.

Working with both Toms (Wilner and Martin) and Jobie was the perfect scenario for an attorney who needed a boost in self-confidence at work during a time when her confidence in general was not exactly at an all-time high. I had thrown myself into my work wholeheartedly because of the heartache and conflict that I was experiencing in my home life with Doug (which didn't necessarily end when the relationship did). The two Toms and Jobie had recognized something in me. They pushed me hard to recognize that I was a smart lawyer and a strong person. It was my task to live up to their expectations, and, more importantly, to my own.

9

A Different Kind of Civil War

MOVING TO WASHINGTON INSTEAD OF NEW YORK WAS supposed to bring Doug and me closer as a couple; I could have
my career and still have time to spend with him, and he could
certainly find a good law job of his own in D.C. that would
pay a decent salary and allow him some free time as well. I
pictured us having dinner at D.C.'s great restaurants, going to
the Kennedy Center, spending hours at the Smithsonian, and
finally enjoying the life together that we'd both worked so hard
to achieve.

The reality of our first few years of married life, however,
was far from what I'd imagined. We rented a little townhouse
apartment out in the Franconia-Springfield area. Doug would
drive me to the metro station each morning, and I'd ride the
train thirty minutes to work, where I would spend the next ten
to twelve hours. Yes, my schedule in Shearman's D.C. office *was*
much more conducive to having a life than if we'd ended up in
New York, but often, even in my first "welcome-to-the-firm"
months, I'd work past eight o' clock, which meant the firm or
the client would buy me dinner and a taxi ride home. I figured
a few late nights wouldn't be a big deal; after all, Doug was busy
looking for a job, and with his great education, which coincidentally was exactly the same as mine (bachelor's degree from

Columbia and Juris Doctorate from UT), it was only a matter of time until he landed himself a job that was likely to be just as demanding.

"This is Kristine," I said into the phone, glancing at the clock. I was amazed to see that it was already seven forty-five.

"Hey, it's me," he said, sounding a little peeved. "What are we doing for dinner?"

"What do you mean?" I asked, trying to force him to spell out what he was really asking. I had been working all day while he was home doing who knows what, and he was asking me what *we* were doing for dinner? I didn't wait for an answer.

"I don't know, Doug," I said, trying not to sound exasperated. "*I'm* working. I've got a stack of things that need my attention before my meeting first thing tomorrow, and I really can't get out of here until it's done. I'll just have some cold cereal when I get home. What are *you* going to do?" I was angry that he was even asking me the question, and I couldn't resist trying to make him feel guilty and throwing some innuendos in my tone and language.

"Okay, great," Doug responded, heavy on the sarcasm. "I guess I'll just throw something together here by myself, then."

"Sounds good, honey," I said. "I'll call you when I'm on my way home."

A few hours and several handfuls of trail mix later, I dialed the number for a taxi (already memorized), grabbed the voucher, and headed home. Just a few steps inside the front door and up the stairs, I came to a quick halt when I got a glance at the kitchen. Dirty dishes were stacked in the sink, and laundry was piled in a messy heap on the living room floor; while Doug may have had good intentions, he never carried the piles to the washing machine twenty feet away. I sighed, hearing the sounds of Doug's current favorite video game coming from the alcove he used as an office.

"Hi," I said, bending down to give him a kiss. He was still wearing the ratty sweatpants and T-shirt he'd been wearing when he drove me to the Metro that morning. *What has he been doing all day?* I didn't say it out loud. The twenty-five minute taxi ride home had calmed me down somewhat, and I was ready to be loving and supportive instead of bitter and mean as I had been on the phone. "Did you find any good job prospects?" I asked sincerely.

Doug's response was a smile in my general direction; he was still focused on his video game.

"I'm exhausted," I said, realizing as the words came out of my mouth that I really meant them. "I think I'm going to forgo the gourmet Cheerios and just go to bed. Are you coming?"

"I'll be down later," Doug answered. He hadn't taken his eyes from the video game once.

It wasn't always that way; some nights I'd get home earlier, around eight or nine, and Doug would've made a nice dinner, done the dishes, showered, and been excited about some of the firms he'd sent his résumé to that day. But as time dragged on, and weeks went by with few interviews and zero job offers, Doug started to get depressed. His depression grew with each failed résumé mailing. Months passed, and we were still at square one—Doug was jobless, I was working feverishly, and things between us were strained. We'd been seeing a marriage counselor since just before we'd been married because we thought it was a good idea (especially given our tenuous relationship early on), but soon it started to seem like a necessity instead of something we did to keep our marriage strong. The weight of being responsible for everything—the car, the house, the dog we had gotten a year earlier in Texas when our relationship started going downhill and we thought it might bring us closer together, the food, our happiness, Doug's unhappiness at moving to D.C.—was growing heavier on me. And the worse things got at home, the more I worked late and during the weekends. I gave in easily to the "big law firm" hours and the perceived demands of the EMLICO case. We spent little time together and I did not protest. Doug never said to me, outright, that it was my fault—that I was the one who'd decided we should move to D.C., and it was because of my decision that he couldn't find a job—but I took on that guilt nonetheless.

Now, I like to think that if I'd been the one without a job, I would've tried harder, taken any job—even a non-legal job I was less than thrilled with—because I couldn't have imagined not contributing to our household in at least some way. But it's always easier to say what one would have done than to actually be the one to do it. I think it was hard for Doug to not have lots of job offers to choose from, and it was also difficult for him to accept that I had such a coveted job at a top law firm when he didn't. The summer we spent in New York right before we were married, he said to me, "I hope you aren't much more successful than me. You're already more successful; I just hope it isn't too much more. It would be hard for me to handle."

Doug was always brutally honest, even when it came to his own feelings. He wasn't used to having to work hard to achieve things: He'd easily been accepted to a top college on the basis of his SATs; he was then awarded a full scholarship to attend a top law school, again, on the basis of his LSAT scores. He didn't feel the need to study much to get decent grades, and didn't hesitate to point that out, to me and to others. I suppose his strategy largely failed him at UT; his grades, while just above a B, were clearly not considered "decent" by Washington, D.C., law firm standards.

Eventually, Doug started doing some volunteer legal work, to have some legal experience to put on his résumé, and just the few hours a day he would spend doing that work seemed to lift a little of his depression. But more months passed and still no job. I couldn't understand it; my frustration grew, and our fights, which by then had turned into screaming matches, became a regular part of our lives.

One day I really lost control of myself.

"You remember my friend, Ken?" Doug asked hesitantly (which was quite unlike him).

"Of course," I responded.

"Well, he's taking a two-week trip to Italy, without Michelle . . . and I was thinking I could meet him there." It was a statement, albeit with something like a question mark at the end.

"Doug," I said, speaking slowly and trying to keep the anger from entering my voice, "you just went to New York. Do you know how hard it was for me to take care of our home and Chili (our dog) too and still do my job at Shearman?"

"I think it would be good for my mind-set," he responded weakly.

Mind-set? "I work ten or twelve hours a day and you want to go to Italy to hang out with your friend and work on your *mind-set*?" I said through gritted teeth. I was furious and couldn't hold back any longer. "What is up with *that*?"

"I'm depressed, Kristine. I am losing it here." Doug's voice was rising in decibel level to match mine. "And, well, frankly . . . I'm kind of bored, too."

"If you are bored, get a fucking job!" I screamed. I started crying and shaking at the same time. Chili had come to sit beside me. He was visibly shaking, too. Doug never went to Italy, at least while we were together.

Despite the knock-down, drag-out fights we had, we somehow managed to stay together. We weren't giving up. Yet. Desperate to do anything to cement our marriage, we bought a little row house on Perry Place (my salary paid for it, as Doug still had no paying job). It was located off Michigan Avenue, in northeast D.C. I hoped that the change of scenery and some home improvement projects would keep Doug busy and help pull him out of his funk. It worked for a while; Doug spent a lot of time working on the house, and he was proud of his new hardwood floors and the pass-through he put in between the kitchen and dining room. I was proud of him, too.

For those few shimmering moments, after we'd moved and Doug had started to contribute something positive, I thought that maybe we'd be okay. But then, somehow, it all just fell apart. He still didn't have a job, and he was still depressed. We still fought all the time. I worked even more hours to avoid the fights, even spending some nights on the floor in my office. I felt that it was preferable to a nightlong fight at home. A couple of nights I snoozed in my car blocks away from our row house. And then, six months or so after we'd moved into the new house, Doug got a real, bona fide lawyer job. It wasn't a "big firm" job like he'd hoped, but a position at a two-person family law firm in Dupont. Nonetheless, it was a job. I should have been elated. Instead, I just felt relieved. For me, it was too little, too late.

A few weeks later, I asked for a separation.

"Kristine," Doug began, "I just got a job. Things are going to get better. You just have to give it some time."

"I *have* given it some time," I said. "It's been almost two years since we moved here. I don't see how your job can fix how broken things are between us." I tried to soften my tone. "Doug, we don't make each other better people. That's what marriage is supposed to do. It's not your fault. It's us, together; *we* don't work. We ought to just try a separation and see how that goes."

The night we officially decided to separate, we slept in separate bedrooms. The next morning, Doug drank his coffee with a determined expression on his face. I knew that look all too well; he was about to drop a bomb.

"Well, Kristine," he said, almost congenially, "I was all ready to move out, and I was even looking in this morning's paper for a place to live, but then I realized that the only thing I could afford were one-room rentals in seedy neighborhoods. You're the one who wants to separate . . . *You* leave."

I was stunned. When we got married, I had jumped in wholeheartedly. Everything we'd bought with my salary belonged to both of us, in my mind; marriage was not some system of loans and paybacks. I'd paid for our food and our other bills; I'd plunked down the cash for our down payment, and then our monthly mortgage payments. I'd paid for our wedding, and I didn't have a problem with it; I truly believed that when you're married, you're in it as a team, and that each spouse makes contributions based on his or her circumstances. Sometimes they are monetary; sometimes they are taking care of the home or children or something else. I'd had faith that someday, Doug would get a job or contribute in some other way and it would all equal out. And if it didn't, so what! We were married. We were a family.

When it didn't end up that way—when I decided to leave "the team," and Doug, who was finally earning a paycheck, asked me to leave the home that my salary alone had bought for us—I was too shocked and guilt-ridden to disagree. The truth is, he was right: I *was* the one who'd asked for the separation, and the house did belong to us both, equally. Or at least, that's what I reminded myself when I quickly moved out and rented a furnished apartment. I continued to pay my rent and our mortgage, our car payment, and both of our student loans.

At first, we were just going to try the separation, to see if a little space was all we needed to realize that we still loved each other. It took less than a few months for it to become clear to me that a separation wasn't going to bring us back together. Doug had a job; he could take care of himself. What we needed, what *I* wanted, was a divorce.

Breaking the news to Doug was tough. He wanted reconciliation but I had made up my mind—and that's when the real trouble began. How to divide up our possessions? In the back of my mind, I thought Doug might just pack up his personal items and leave. But Doug had a different idea: Everything should be split down the middle. I didn't protest; it was a fair division. Doug's math, however, made it clear that "down the middle" was a phrase subject to interpretation. The amount of fighting we did over the value of the house, the car, the furniture, everything we owned, was bitterly painful, nauseating, and time-consuming. My friends told me I should fight it out in court, because no judge in her right mind would find in Doug's favor.

I was tired of fighting. Truthfully, I didn't want to take him to court. I knew that would only prolong the fighting, and in the end, I did consider everything we'd acquired during our marriage to be half his. Meanwhile, I was still working a demanding schedule at Shearman, and I needed, wanted, to be able to focus on work, not the death of my marriage. In the end, Doug kept the furniture. He kept the house. I got the Ford Escort and fifteen thousand dollars for my half of the house, to be paid in two installments. The divorce was finalized in 2001, after four years of marriage including the year we were separated, and not a moment too soon.

I'd been training for a marathon in the months leading up to the divorce, even during several intense months of the EMLICO case. I'd always wanted to run a marathon, and with all of the upheaval in my life, I needed something positive to focus on. I ran the marathon the weekend after the EMLICO team, including me, spent two weeks in the Waldorf-Astoria in New York doing the EMLICO arbitration, pulling an all-nighter two days before the race and eating pretzels for dinner on a few occasions.

The Marine Corps Marathon 2001 was less than two months after 9/11. The race was fraught with emotion, as everyone feared another terrorist attack would take place during an event with big crowds that included numerous American servicemen and -women. Additionally, the course took the runners right past the Pentagon, which at that time was still scarred by a big black gash. Although green military helicopters hovered in the skies to ensure our safety, we were still nervous that morning, wondering if we would be killed in a terrorist attack (or if our bodies would fail us at mile twenty-four). My sister came down from New York to cheer me on, even running several portions of the race with me. And Laura Blood, my pal from law school who was living in D.C. at the time, walked the last mile with me. (I was *running* that last mile, but VERY slowly.) I crossed the finish line at a faster clip. I had done it!

My race was the weekend before Doug and I met in court to finalize our divorce. I was proudly limping. The whole thing, from running the marathon, to showing up in court for my divorce, was fantastic, cathartic, and the beginning of a new life for me. Training for and finishing a twenty-six-mile foot race is one of the best ways to show yourself that you can endure anything if you put your mind to it. I got through a marathon with no problem; I was going to get through the divorce and be just fine.

After the judge had finalized the divorce, I sped away from the courthouse in my newly acquired little Audi TT convertible, music pumping, singing at the top of my lungs, wanting to put as much distance as possible between me and the divorce. I felt completely unburdened for about one mile—until I got pulled over for speeding on Washington Boulevard in Arlington.

"You were going a little bit fast for this area," the cop said. She looked a little unnerved at my broad smile. I suppose most drivers greet a speeding ticket with a frown. On any other day, I would have as well.

"I am so sorry," I said, still grinning. "I just got a divorce!" I blurted out gleefully. "I am so happy. Bring on the ticket. Honestly, I really don't care."

She laughed. And then she wrote me the ticket.

10

Into Guantánamo

I COULD NEVER HAVE PREDICTED, WHEN I FIRST STARTED AT Shearman, that I would be called into Tom Wilner's office and asked what I thought about a situation that had been presented to him by a group of Kuwaiti families: They feared their sons had been picked up by the U.S. government and were possibly being held in a military detention center at Guantánamo Bay, Cuba. Even after our conversation, I couldn't have known how life-changing this case would become for me—that it would place me on an unstoppable trajectory that would eventually define my career.

I had finally started to come into my own as a lawyer, but I couldn't have realized that I was about to embark on a journey that would become a great passion of mine. It would fill a hole inside me that had existed ever since I took the career counselor's advice at UT and applied for summer associate programs at various big-time law firms, "just to see" what might be out there. Before I stepped off that precipice, I had been a hard-charging girl from New York, something of a radical among my fellow law students at UT, interested in public interest law and willing to fight authority.

This did not necessarily make me a die-hard liberal. I wasn't then, and am not now. When I speak about my work with the detainees at Guantánamo, I am careful to say up front that my parents were in the U.S. Army, that my dad fought in Vietnam, and that both of my grandfathers fought for the United States in World War II. Sometimes I mention that before the 2008 primaries, I was registered to vote as a Libertarian. I even joke that some of my best friends are Republican. In truth, I am surrounded by Republicans: My parents vote Republican; Laura Blood, my dear law school friend, is a Republican; and, also, my boyfriend through the six years of my Guantánamo representation (who is now my husband) is a *staunch* (with a capital "S") Republican. In short, I like Republicans. Without explicitly saying so, I tell my audiences not to write me off simply because I think prisoners held by our American government have a right to counsel and a fair trial, that they too have a right to "justice," even if they have been accused of terrible acts. I did not get involved with this case out of a desire to promote liberal values. I simply felt then (and still feel now) that it was the right thing to do. And it all began on September 11, 2001.

I was in New York City when the World Trade Center was attacked, a death-filled event of historic proportions now referred to as simply "9/11," as if real words are incapable of capturing the tragedy. Tom Martin, Jobie, and I were staying at the Waldorf-Astoria, smack in the middle of our umpteenth arbitration hearing on EMLICO. The Shearman team and its co-counsel, Chadbourne & Parke (coincidentally), had rented out a large suite at the Waldorf so that we could set up a little law firm away from home. We'd trucked in hundreds of binders filled with documents and exhibits for our witnesses' testimonies, setting them up on rows of rented shelves next to conference tables and work stations in our suite. Other than the beautiful molding around the floorboards and ceiling and the extremely expensive room service, it almost looked like a law firm office; we called it our "war room." We also had a few side rooms where we could meet with our witnesses or clients away from the din of the war room.

The arbitration hearing was held in another large suite at the Waldorf, which had been cleared of all hotel furniture and arranged with conference tables to simulate a courtroom. The proceedings always started promptly at nine each morning, but the worker bees (me, other associates, the paralegals, etc.) usually gathered at seven-thirty or earlier to begin preparing for the day.

September eleventh started like any other day. We were busy collecting the documents, exhibits, and other items we'd need for the day's arbitration. Tom and Jobie eventually rolled in, Tom his usual grim self, and Jobie, talkative and smiling, getting the team pumped up for the long day's hearing. At around ten minutes to nine, we began packing up the exhibit binders to take to the hearing room, when Peter, one of our clients, burst into the room. He reported in his perfect Bermudian accent that "some idiot had just run his plane into the World Trade Center," and that we should turn on the TV.

We turned on the television to watch the breaking news coverage from our hotel in midtown Manhattan, less than four miles away from where the scene was actually unfolding. At first we watched with casual interest; every station was showing the same image—one of the towers with a black gaping hole, billowing smoke. The details were sketchy, and some news anchors were still indicating that reports of a plane hitting the tower were "unconfirmed." *Poor schmuck (or idiot)*, we all thought. We had no idea that a commercial airliner carrying hundreds of passengers had flown directly into the World Trade Center. The newscasters were uncertain as to the size or type of plane; some eyewitnesses stated it was a small plane, while others said the explosion definitely came from inside the tower.

By nine a.m., all of the channels were focused on the two towers, with the voices of eyewitnesses in the background providing bits and pieces of information. At three minutes after nine, we all watched the second plane hit the south tower; on television, the plane looked small, like a Cessna, but the explosion (and the fireball that came off the building) was huge. News anchors, normally cool and collected, cried out "Oh my God!" on the air. The fear in their voices was unnerving. We were all riveted to the television; any thoughts of our impending arbitration had vanished. We watched people jump out of the first tower—a sight I will never forget—knowing that this was actually happening just miles away. We couldn't tear ourselves away from the images of the two towers and the smoke that blanketed lower Manhattan.

Then came the breaking news that there had been an explosion and fire at the Pentagon; reports were uncertain as to the cause.

I felt sick to my stomach. *Did I know anybody who worked at the Pentagon?* That was close to my apartment, less than two miles away. Reports came rushing out of Washington in a jumble: The Mall was on fire (*Oh God, that's down the block from the Shearman office*), the White House and the Capitol were being evacuated (*Elaine! My friend Elaine is working on the Hill! I'm sure she's okay; she's tough*). We remained glued to the chaos on the screen. An hour after the first attack, although it seemed like minutes, we saw the south tower come sliding down, starting from the top, slowly at first, then picking up speed and crashing into a smoldering, gigantic pile of concrete, glass, papers, and bodies. The north tower—the building that was hit first—collapsed thirty minutes later.

The only one to speak was the partner from Chadbourne. He turned to the group around the TV, numb and in shock, and asked, "So . . . was that one occurrence, or two?" His brain must have tried to seize on something familiar to him, something technical so that he wouldn't have to process what was really happening. In the insurance industry, coverage is often based on the number of occurrences. The partner was wondering aloud whether each hit was a separate occurrence, or whether the entire event—the two planes colliding into the two towers of the World Trade Center—made up one larger occurrence. (It would make a huge difference in the way the insurance company would pay out the claim, and it would eventually become the subject of a complex and expensive litigation.)

The experience felt surreal. Many of us, including me, were crying as we watched, while others were shocked into silence. We were all horrified.

My cell phone rang, shaking me out of my stupor. Kim's work number at Judson Grill, a midtown restaurant less than ten blocks away, popped up on the display. "Kim?!" I cried, wanting to hear her voice.

"Yes, it's me. I'm fine. I'm at work. Are you okay? I tried to call your office when I heard the Pentagon had been hit, but Maria told me you were here, in New York. Where are you?" Kim's voice rose to a high pitch at the end. I hadn't told her yet that I was in New York. Since I traveled there so often, sometimes I'd tell her only after I'd arrived and knew when I'd have some free time to stop by and see her. She sounded as dazed as I felt. I'm sure I sounded the same way to her.

"I'm fine. I'm at the Waldorf again," I heard myself say. "I'm going to call Mom and Dad."

"Okay. Be careful—and call me later. I love you," Kim said.

"You too," I repeated. "Love you."

I knew my parents wouldn't be awake yet; it was just after ten in the morning in New York, but in Alaska it was only six. My mom answered on the first ring, her voice thick with sleep.

"Mom," I said, trying to sound as confident as possible. "Umm . . . when you go to work this morning, you're going to hear some news—bad things are happening in New York and Washington, but Kim and I are just fine, okay? We are good. I just wanted to let you know. Go listen to the news. It's not good."

"Okay," Mom responded easily. I knew she wouldn't really comprehend what I was saying until after she was truly awake, but I also knew she would've been frantic to reach her girls if I hadn't called. My cell phone rang again. It was Laura in D.C. She knew I was in New York for two weeks.

"Kristine? I can't believe I got a hold of you. Are you all right?" she stumbled over her words, obviously anxious. "I can't get a hold of Danielle," Laura said without waiting for my answer. Danielle, her sister, lived downtown, near the World Trade Center. I was touched that she'd called to check on me, but felt helpless where Danielle was concerned. "I'm sure she's fine," I said. "She doesn't work in the towers, right? She's probably already evacuated the area, and is someplace safe." I was trying to think of anything to say that would help Laura feel better. Laura found out hours later that her sister was safe. I can't imagine what those hours must have felt like, having a sister myself.

None of us could make or receive any other calls that day. Somehow, I'd managed to speak with both my sister and my mom before the lines got jammed.

Finally, after hours in front of the TV, watching the same gut-wrenching footage of people jumping and the eventual collapse of the towers, mass evacuations in D.C., and listening as the news anchors fed us details about the plane crash in Pennsylvania, someone on my team said, "I can't take this. We have to get out of here. Let's take a walk." By then, many of the lawyers and legal assistants on both teams had drifted back to their rooms in the hotel, to try to reach their families, or cry in private, or perhaps have a stiff drink. Getting some fresh air sounded like a good idea to me. I couldn't watch any more.

Roland, another colleague from the EMLICO case, and I went out on the streets of Manhattan around noon on 9/11. It was eerie, like an episode from *The Twilight Zone*. There were a few people on the streets, but no cars other than the parked ones. Less than two hours after the attack, every entrance to the island had been shut down. By Manhattan standards, it was completely silent. We looked down Sixth Avenue, and it was empty, all the way downtown.

We were about sixty or seventy blocks from the towers, probably about three and a half miles. We couldn't see the buildings, but we saw big plumes of smoke, and people on rooftops trying to get a view of what was happening. The few people on the streets looked to be in shock, as we must have looked; some people cried openly as they walked by. We decided to go to the Red Cross on the West Side to see if we could donate blood, since it was close. We weren't the only ones with that idea—the place was completely packed with people, and there was a line around the block, all wanting to donate blood. It was incredibly touching to see all of these eager New Yorkers lined up, hoping to help somehow, and to hear the staffers greeting us: "Please go somewhere else to donate; we have more than enough donors here."

From there, I walked to my sister's apartment on the Upper West Side; she opened the door, we saw each other, and immediately started crying and hugging. I spent about an hour with her before I headed back to the hotel. We cut the arbitration short and headed home the next day, but because the airports in D.C. and New York were still in lockdown, we ended up taking a train from New York back to D.C., stopping several times on account of bomb scares and other delays.

For a while afterward, life for me back in D.C. returned to almost normal. I jumped back into my work, and although there were no more EMLICO hearings for a while, I was also working on the Mexican tomato case and finishing the OPEC work.

Then, in March of 2002, less than six months after that fateful fall morning in New York, my life took a turn. "I have received a kind of a strange request," Tom Wilner said. He'd called me into his office for a chat, which wasn't particularly unusual; it was his request that intrigued me.

"I'm sure you've been asked many strange things in your lifetime, Tom. I don't want to hear anything really weird or kinky, okay?" I said, jokingly. Tom and I had gotten to know each other pretty well over the past year, and I knew he would appreciate my humor, but his look was serious that morning. I dropped the ribbing. "Let's hear it."

"I got a referral," he continued. "Shearman was approached by an American lawyer and a Kuwaiti lawyer. There is a group of Kuwaiti families who want us to do an investigation of sorts . . . There are some Kuwaitis—sons of the families—who are missing. They went to Afghanistan, Pakistan, and Iran, or somewhere, and haven't been heard from since we invaded Afghanistan. I don't know for sure; it wasn't clear what really happened. That's why they've asked us to get involved."

"Uh-huh," I said. We'd invaded Afghanistan five months earlier, in October of 2001, and although like most Americans I was concerned about what our troops were facing overseas, I really hadn't been paying much attention to the details. "Isn't this a matter for a private detective, or an investigator? Why us?" I asked.

"The families have asked us to see if we can determine whether their sons are in U.S. custody," he said. "They want us to help confirm their whereabouts, find out under whose or what jurisdiction, department, or agency they are being held. If it's the U.S., the families will take it from there—but they need some help to get either a confirmation or a 'no' from our government. They may end up needing criminal defense lawyers, if their sons are being prosecuted for some crime. We can advise them on that, but we are not obligated to continue representing them."

"Interesting," I said, thinking that it sounded fairly simple and straightforward; we'd ask the U.S. government to confirm or deny that the Kuwaiti men were being held by the American government, hand over the info to the Kuwaiti families, and be done with it. We had connections in the government, or at least Tom did. At the time, it hadn't really occurred to me that this group of men might actually be at Guantánamo. I hadn't been paying much attention to the Guantánamo issue at that point—no one really was. It was barely mentioned in the newspaper. "What's the catch?"

"Well," Tom said slowly, "I haven't decided whether or not to take the case. I was approached by a Kuwaiti lawyer who went to an American friend for advice. They were directed to us, as a D.C. law firm with governmental experience. What do you think about it?"

"We're not criminal defense lawyers, but it doesn't sound like that's what they need. It does seem rather intriguing," I said, matching Tom's thoughtful tone. "I'm in."

We wouldn't find out until months later that the Kuwaitis had approached nine other D.C.–area law firms before contacting us. They'd been turned down by every other well-known law firm in the District, their case deemed "too controversial."

The next day, Tom stopped by my office to report the verdict: He'd decided to take the case, and he wondered if I was still willing to help. As always, I was up for anything that involved working with either of the two Toms, international clients, and some travel. This case looked like it would involve all three. It wasn't a criminal case; it was all about putting the Kuwaiti families in touch with the right people. In our minds, and in the minds of the Kuwaitis, once we'd confirmed that their sons *were* being held by the U.S., it would all work out. This was America, after all, and America didn't have such a thing as "ghost prisoners"—people secretly held in prison by the government. I had learned that the Chinese government had them during my pro bono representation of a Tibetan man claiming political asylum. But our State Department had called that a "human rights abuse." That's not how *we* operated. We didn't even use the term *ghost prisoner* before 9/11.

Our first order of business was to travel to Kuwait and meet the families to get a sense of who our clients were, who exactly was missing, where and why they had been traveling, and why and how they may have been picked up by the U.S.

We knew very little before going to Kuwait, other than the fact that the Kuwaitis we were representing may have been picked up in Afghanistan by U.S. military forces. There was also vague speculation that Guantánamo somehow figured into the puzzle. To prepare before our flight to Kuwait City, I put together a binder of every recent news article I could find on U.S. detentions in Afghanistan and Guantánamo, which really wasn't much. Almost every article mentioned that people being held at Guantánamo were considered "illegal enemy combatants," a somewhat new term created by the Bush administration, and that the Geneva Conventions were at issue. *Geneva Conventions? What in the hell . . . ?*

I'd never been involved in international law like this before. I mean, I had been exposed to Bermuda and English law during the EMLICO hearings, and I always said I practiced "international litigation and arbitration." (It sounded good, and that's what our practice group was called.) But I didn't really do *international* law, like UN stuff, and I sure as hell didn't know anything about the Geneva Conventions! To that end, I'd also printed out the Geneva Conventions to read over during the flight.

In early news reports, according to the White House, the Geneva Conventions applied to Taliban prisoners but not to al-Qaeda members. Later news reports clarified that the administration's position was that the protections of the Conventions didn't apply to anyone at Guantánamo because they were not "prisoners of war"—they were enemy combatants. The "spirit" of the Conventions would be followed, nonetheless. *Well, that's nice. But what does that really mean?* I found myself intrigued. Working on a case that involved the Geneva Conventions was something I'd never even considered an option at Shearman & Sterling.

When Tom and I arrived in Kuwait, we were greeted by "Mr. B," an American and former partner at Sullivan and Cromwell. At that time Mr. B was working in Abu Dhabi and was well known in the Middle East as a prominent American lawyer. We met with Mr. B to gain some insight into Kuwaiti culture and the families we were about to meet before being introduced to Abdul Rahman Al-Haroun, the Kuwaiti lawyer representing the families.

Mr. B, although polite enough, came from the "school of important law firms," where partners don't necessarily talk to associates as if they are equals. He spoke mainly to Tom, until Tom made it clear in both tone and gesture that the two of us came as a package deal. Mr. B then turned to me. "First of all, Kristine," he said, "don't offer to shake Abdul Rahman's hand; he probably won't shake yours. In fact, don't shake the hand of any male unless they offer theirs first."

My mind flashed back to my middle school experiences in Saudi Arabia. I had been thinking about my time in the Middle East before we'd left for Kuwait, agonizing over what clothing to bring. I finally decided on loose, long-sleeved shirts, long skirts, a baggy suit from Ann Taylor, and a shawl that could cover my head, just in case. I knew Kuwait was considered more progressive than Saudi, but still, I was a little nervous about meeting the Kuwaitis, including the lawyer. Mr. B said the lawyer traveled to the U.S. all the time; he also told me that it wasn't necessary for me to wear a scarf. All the same, I was still nervous about Abdul Rahman's reaction to working with a female lawyer.

We met Abdul Rahman for breakfast, right before our meeting with the families. He shook Mr. B's and Tom's hands, but not mine. It didn't bother me, as he was exceptionally polite and treated me as part of the team. He was actually a lot nicer to me than a lot of partners I'd met from well-known American law firms. We walked down the hallway to the hotel's conference room—Tom, a fifty-eight-year-old balding Jewish man; Mr. B, an older white man in a classic Western-style suit; Abdul Rahman, older also, in a classic Middle Eastern white thobe and headdress; and me, a thirty-four-year-old half-Filipino female in a baggy Ann Taylor suit—about to introduce ourselves to a group of Muslim Kuwaitis. Talk about a study in diversity!

We entered the conference room and found the families seated around a big square table. Or, rather, the men of the families were seated around the table. *Of course*, I thought, *the women wouldn't come.* I was the sole woman in a group of almost twenty men, two white guys in suits, and about fifteen or so Arab men in Muslim garb—the fathers and brothers of the missing Kuwaitis. Abdul Rahman introduced us in English, and I took a deep breath. If we'd been in the U.S., we'd have made the rounds, shaking everyone's hands, saying our names, handing out business cards, and smiling. Here, there were few smiles, no shaking of hands, just solemn looks. We took our seats at one end of the table and let Abdul Rahman do the talking.

After introducing Mr. B., Tom, and me by name, and briefly explaining our backgrounds, he got right to the point. "Over the next few days," he said, "we'll meet with each family to learn the particulars about each Kuwaiti citizen. We'll also be meeting with somebody in the Foreign Ministry." I could see some of the men whispering in translation to others. I was used to that, having represented plenty of non-English-speaking clients before. There wasn't much else to say. At that point, none of us knew what we were facing, much less what we were planning to do. None of us could have guessed, at that point, what was happening to their sons and brothers in Guantánamo as we sat around that table.

The next few days in Kuwait were filled with meetings with the families. We met often with one of the fathers in particular, Khalid Al-Odah, who became our main contact and the representative for all of the families. Khalid's son Fawzi was one of those who'd gone missing, just twenty-three years old when he'd left Kuwait. We spent a lot of time with Khalid, getting a sense of what he knew and had already learned, which turned out to be a lot more than we had first realized.

When Fawzi went missing, Khalid had taken action, just like any father would have. He began knocking on doors, trying to meet with government officials who could help and trying to find other families with similar experiences. The majority of the Kuwaiti families we were meeting with had not known each other before their sons or brothers disappeared. They'd found each other by word of mouth. Once they had started inquiring, they learned of the Kuwaiti Family Committee, formed by Khalid, for the families of Kuwaiti detainees at Guantánamo.

Basically, the stories were similar: A young man would leave Kuwait for Afghanistan, Pakistan, or Iran, individually and at various times, some before 9/11, some after, either to volunteer in humanitarian aid efforts, to assist refugees, or to perform some other kind of charitable service, as is mandated by Muslim religion. Even before 9/11, there had been a significant and protracted amount of fighting in Afghanistan between the Taliban, the Northern Alliance, and ethnic groups. Civil war and the slaughter of thousands of civilians by the Taliban led to a huge refugee movement in and out of Afghanistan, to the borders of and into Pakistan and Iran. For many Afghans, assistance from the outside was a necessity.

The Kuwaiti citizens had left Kuwait to volunteer with various aid organizations, and had been in contact with their families regularly—until the U.S. invasion of Afghanistan. Some of the families lost contact with their sons/brothers directly after the invasion, others shortly thereafter. Some families had heard that the U.S. military was holding people in Pakistan and at the U.S. military base in Bagram, Afghanistan, and that their sons might be among those prisoners. Other families had gotten unconfirmed reports from the Red Cross that their sons were being held at Guantánamo. The Red Cross transmits mail from prison camps in areas of conflict to the family members of the prisoners. One father even had a Red Cross letter with GUANTÁNAMO stamped on it; most of the words from his son were blacked out, presumably by censors.

It was suspected that a total of twelve Kuwaiti citizens were being held at Guantánamo, but the families couldn't confirm the rumors. Khalid had personally gone to the U.S. Embassy in Kuwait and asked the Americans to confirm whether his son and the sons of the other families were at Gitmo, only to have his request refused outright. The families had banded together to try every angle, and by the time Tom and I arrived, the families had already paved the way for us to meet with the Kuwait Foreign Ministry.

Unfortunately, we learned very little. The U.S. Embassy had only recently revealed to the Kuwait Foreign Ministry that there were five Kuwaiti citizens currently being held at Gitmo. The only other information they provided was a list of their names and the date that each was brought to Guantánamo. There were no reasons given for the detainment, no information about the citizens' health or other status, no mention of charges, no indication of what the U.S. planned on doing with these men. Nothing. And by the time Tom and I arrived in Kuwait, the families' sons had been missing for more than four or five months, without confirmation that they were dead or alive.

The families were desperate for any information—just to know where their sons were would have been a major relief for them, especially since America had invaded Afghanistan and was officially at war. The families were worried their sons might be dead.

Along with meeting the families, Tom, Abdul Rahman, Khalid, and I met with the various charitable organizations that some of the missing men had been associated with; we wanted to get an idea of what the organizations were like, and what kind of work the men had been doing. For those meetings, Khalid kindly requested that I wear my scarf and be completely silent. (We'd only been working together a few days, but he already had a sense of my personality.) I had no problem agreeing to his terms, and sat about twenty feet away from the men, close enough so that I could still hear what they were saying. I didn't say a word; I just sat in the corner, listened, and observed. In the U.S., I wouldn't have been okay with this arrangement, but in Kuwait, I was fine with it. I didn't feel the need to act upon my feminist principles in that situation. I'd had the good fortune of being able to work with people of different cultures at Shearman; I'd also traveled extensively, and lived in some pretty exotic lands. I may be brazen and outspoken, but I also know that using good judgment is one of the best traits an effective lawyer can have. Afterward, Khalid laughed, saying, "Wow, that was really demure for you!"

Meetings with the families were a lot less cautious for me. They had to be, since Tom put me in charge while he went off to track down another meeting with the Foreign Ministry or some other Kuwaiti governmental agency. The families—that is, the men—didn't really have a choice: There was me . . . and then there was me. I met with each family individually, with Khalid translating for the father or brother who didn't speak English. Although Kuwait is a pretty progressive country, the population is still Muslim, and we were still in the Middle East, which meant that the more traditionally thinking families were a little less open to speaking to or in front of me than others were.

At the beginning, some of them wouldn't look at me, and they would barely speak to me; they seemed to be talking to Khalid or to the window across the room, which was particularly awkward because I was trying to get them to answer questions about their sons, when they went missing, and other details that we might need to help them. Usually, by the end of the conversation, whoever was talking to me—father, brother, cousin—would be speaking passionately about their relative and looking me in the eye with something akin to hope and deep sadness. It was clear they would give anything to be reunited with their loved one. They showed me pictures, talked about their sons' likes and dislikes, their sons' children—sharing with me anything they thought might be helpful.

On our last day, Khalid and Abdul Rahman took us to lunch at a famous rotating restaurant at the top of Liberation Tower, completed in 1996 in commemoration of the country's liberation from Iraq, which had, of course, been largely assisted by the U.S. Khalid had been a pilot in the Kuwaiti Air Force and had fought next to Americans in the first Gulf War. Khalid recounted that when the American soldiers had rolled into Kuwait City in their tanks, Fawzi, who was thirteen years old at the time, had run out into the streets, shouting with joy and waving an American flag. Fawzi loved America. Khalid had such faith in America, in the American system of justice, that he was relieved to have discovered his son might be in U.S. custody.

"I thought, when I found out my son was in Guantánamo, or in custody of the U.S.," he began, "I said, 'Thanks to Allah. Because my son will be all right.' "

Little did we know then that being in U.S. custody at Guantánamo Bay would turn out to be, for many of our clients, anything but all right, and for Khalid, in particular: Right now, more than seven years later, his son is still there. He has never been charged or given a trial; he has had no physical contact with his father or any member of his family since leaving Kuwait. At that moment, though, Tom and I felt confident that we could do something, as lawyers, to help these people. As we left, thanking Khalid for his patience, and his efforts, he reached out his hand and shook mine.

"I have to shake your hand, Ms. Huskey," he said. "Thank you. Thank *you*."

Suddenly I was crafting another letter home: *Dear Mom: You will not believe the experiences I have had in Kuwait over the last five days.*

Upon our return to D.C., we met with our other teammate on the case, Neil Koslowe, and explained in detail what we'd heard from the Kuwaiti families. Neil had stayed behind in Washington to do a little government digging. He'd worked at the Department of Justice (DOJ) for years and had some contacts that we hoped would be helpful.

"I have to say, it's not looking good," he began. "People are telling me, no, *warning* me not to get involved. If it involves Guantánamo, they're saying, we're not going to get *any* information. I'm hearing that it's completely useless to even try. Even my friends at DOJ don't know what's going on, and if they do, they aren't allowed to tell me. It's like a wall of silence descends when I mention Guantánamo; it's like nothing I've ever experienced." Neil continued: "I have also learned that there have been habeas petitions filed by some organization in New York called CCR, short for the Center for Constitutional Rights, and some death penalty lawyer—Joe Margulies—on behalf of two British citizens and two Australians detained at Guantánamo."

Habeas petitions? Death penalty? A habeas petition is something a prisoner files, usually after he or she's been convicted, to challenge their imprisonment. This wasn't supposed to involve criminal work; what could *we* do? I felt like I was in way over my head, and any hope I'd felt upon leaving Kuwait seemed to be fading fast—until I looked up at Tom and Neil, who looked determined and ready to do something, come hell or high water. I think Neil hated getting the brush-off from his former colleagues; Tom just hated being told no.

"We're going to have to sue the bastards," Tom said. "That's the only way to force them [the U.S. government] to be accountable. They'll have to come forward in some way, to respond. Neil? Kristine? What do you think?"

"I'm in," we responded in unison.

With that, our mission was set. We began to do a lot of legal and factual research to figure out what kind of legal action we should bring, even though we barely knew a thing about the situation, because that's how the U.S. government wanted it. It was like operating in a vacuum: We weren't allowed to talk to our clients; their families weren't allowed to talk to them; the government wouldn't tell us, the families, or the Kuwaiti government anything; and the prisoners were sitting in Cuba in a U.S.-run military prison where no civilians, not even the press, was allowed. The Kuwaitis hadn't been charged with any crime as far as we knew, and clearly they weren't going to be hauled into court anytime soon. Other than the habeas petitions filed by CCR, there were no other lawsuits or lawyers in the U.S. working to represent detainees at Guantánamo.

We began to realize that if we didn't file *something* on behalf of our clients, we were going to miss our opportunity to get in on the litigation. The issues were going to be decided without us, and, more significantly, our clients would be affected by whatever that decision was. We needed to get in on the action, and we needed to do it immediately. We filed on May 1, 2002, eight months after 9/11, and two months after our visit to Kuwait.

Instead of filing a habeas corpus petition, which essentially asks the government official holding a prisoner to prove the validity of the detention or release the prisoner, we filed a traditional complaint, claiming that our clients' due process rights had been violated and that they should be entitled to consult with counsel and their families, and that they should be charged and/or provided with an impartial hearing or trial. It was strategic thinking on our part, because we didn't want to seem as if we were asking the court to release these detainees without some sort of hearing first. By then we knew that they were considered "the worst of the worst" by both the government and the public, but we needed to file something that would force the government to come forward and explain to the court why it was holding people without charges, lawyers, or trial, and without any rights under American or international law. We were sure the court would never go for such a blatant disregard of fundamental rights. Back then, we thought anybody who was reasonable and believed in justice must certainly believe in the notion of due process, at a minimum. How could a judge not rule in favor of due process?

As we had anticipated, the D.C. District Court essentially combined the two cases—the habeas petitions filed by CCR and our due process complaint—and assigned them to the same judge, Colleen Kollar-Kotelly. The government's response was quick and surprising: a motion to dismiss. The motion itself wasn't the shocker; it was the grounds upon which it was based.

The government's brief opened with a description of the horrific events of 9/11 and the fact that we were currently involved in a "global war on terror." It went on to say that the detainees at Guantánamo had been picked up on the "battlefield in Afghanistan," and were enemy combatants. The government's main argument, though, did not depend on those facts, compelling as they were; the government's primary argument was that the U.S. courts had no jurisdiction over the case because the Kuwaiti men were foreign citizens, and the Guantánamo U.S. military base was not technically in the sovereign territory of the United States. Therefore, according to the government, the court had no authority to even hear or review our case, and should immediately dismiss it outright.

Let me get this straight, I thought: Even though the Guantánamo military base is run solely by Americans and, according to the lease between Cuba and Guantánamo, the U.S. has "exclusive custody and control" over Guantánamo and every person there, because Guantánamo isn't somewhere like Idaho, smack dab in the middle of our country, the U.S. government can hold foreigners there virtually incommunicado? Without any due process, or contact with family or legal counsel? Without any way to prove their innocence, or know why they are being held? *This was unbelievable.*

Once the shock had worn off, Tom, Neil, and I wrote back in opposition: "The government's argument has no limits. If the Court accepts the defendants' theory, U.S. officials could do whatever they wanted to foreign nationals held outside the United States, denying them not only the most basic procedural rights of due process, but substantive rights as well, including guarantees against torture." Meaning that under the government's theory, the government could have abducted people off the streets of Rome, held them at a secret site and tortured them, and no court would have the power to review its actions. We argued in the extreme to demonstrate the absurdity of the position. Although at the time we couldn't imagine that our rhetoric could possibly be true, today we know: That's exactly what the Bush administration *had* been doing—running around all over the world, going into people's homes, picking up "suspects," bringing them to Guantánamo and other detention "black sites," and torturing them. Back then, however, we couldn't imagine that our country would ever act so unethically, so immorally, and we couldn't believe a U.S. court would buy into that theory.

Except, the court did. The district court granted the government's motion to dismiss on August 8, 2002.

We were stunned—or maybe just naïve. At least, Tom and I were. Neil was pretty sure we were going to lose, and lose we did, big time. I simply could not believe that the court had decided foreign citizens could be held by the United States, with no authority to ensure that the government would treat its prisoners humanely. We hadn't asked for them to be released. We simply wanted them to have the rights we felt they were owed under the Constitution, the Geneva Conventions, and other human rights treaties. Those rights would then dictate that some sort of process be provided to the prisoners in order to sort out the real terrorists from innocent civilians. And we had been denied.

Even before the district court ruled, Tom and I had already begun, slowly, to realize the scope of what we'd gotten ourselves into. We realized why the Kuwaitis had been turned down by nine other law firms, and why they were so thrilled to have us on board. We were Shearman & Sterling, after all—a New York "white-shoe" law firm (a slang term for a broker-dealer firm that is against hostile takeover practices) with big-name clients like GE, Merrill Lynch, Citibank, and OPEC. We brought a certain respectability to this case that a typical, ultraliberal NGO (nongovernmental organization) like CCR could not.

Many of our own colleagues at Shearman's New York office didn't like what we were doing. Several of them, along with their clients, had been personally affected by 9/11, and, in addition, they didn't want to risk involvement in such a controversial topic that might tarnish the firm's reputation. They wanted us to drop the case, but Tom refused, threatening to quit if he wasn't allowed to continue representing the Kuwaitis. Tom won that fight. Even some of my friends from law school expressed disbelief when they heard I was representing Guantánamo detainees.

"How can you take that case, Kristine?" Laura Blood asked over margaritas on the roof of Lauriol Plaza in Dupont. "They were fighting in Afghanistan. They're terrorists."

"Well, how do we know they are terrorists or were actually fighting, if they haven't had any hearing or trial?" I countered. "Besides, many of them were doing humanitarian work over there and got swooped up."

"And you believe that? What were they doing in Afghanistan during a civil war if it wasn't to fight?" another friend of ours admonished.

"Did you forget that I lived in Angola with a UNICEF aid worker during a civil war? Just because most Americans don't go overseas to volunteer, doesn't mean that others don't." I responded. *Are you assuming these people are guilty until proven innocent?* It was a shocking thought. "Don't you remember law school?" I asked instead.

It was only the first of many debates about the Guantánamo detainees Laura and I would have. Despite her disagreement with me on several fronts, Laura was my best friend in D.C. She continued to support me, even bragging to people about the work that I was doing. She knew it was important work, that it was important to me, and that I was standing up for what I believed, even if she didn't agree with my beliefs. Others were equally encouraging: "You are the man in the white suit," a friend said to me after I had just been challenged about my work (rather aggressively) by her husband, who had also been in Section Three with me during our first year of law school.

"What you're doing . . . that's why we went to law school," Rebecca stated emphatically, smiling sweetly at her husband.

Of course, some people were not as supportive as Laura or Rebecca.

"We're not doing anything wrong by holding these people," a guest of mine once said. It was my own Fourth of July party, and we were standing on my balcony with a perfect view of the fireworks over the Mall. Let freedom ring.

"We can't just hold people in detention, without charging them or providing representation," I said.

"Sure we can. We've done it before, during World War Two," he responded smugly. And he wasn't referring to German prisoners of war.

"Yes, but we look back in history at the internment of Japanese-Americans as being *wrong*, don't we? Or am I missing something here?" I said. I was pissed and wanted to throw him off my balcony.

We were getting it from all sides. Tom received hate e-mails from strangers, the nicest one stating that we should be locked up in Guantánamo with the terrorists. One or two brief articles had appeared in *The Washington Post* about lawyers suing the government for holding unlawful enemy combatants at Guantánamo. Our firm's name (and Tom's) had made it into the public eye.

For me, the entire concept of what patriotism meant had changed. During that time, and for a long time after 9/11, our government was working pretty hard to garner allegiance among its citizens by instilling fear, sending the message loud and clear: "If you're not with us, you're against us." I had found myself on the "against" side, and wondered how I could be against the U.S. for standing up for principles that are traditionally cherished by Americans. I couldn't believe that Americans could be so opposed to the basic ideals that we had memorialized in our Constitution; that they could be opposed to holding the government accountable—and so opposed to offering due process to the human beings in our custody.

With Tom as my mentor, I'd learned that principles don't really matter much in times of peace. It's easy to maintain your ideology when everything is stable and life is good; it's during times of conflict that holding fast to your values really matters. It is conflict that truly tests your beliefs. I believed then (and still believe now) that America is one of the greatest countries in the world—but my faith in our government, and, worse, my faith in my fellow countrymen to stand up for what's right, would be shaken even more over the course of the next several years.

Our team at Shearman had decided to create a three-pronged strategy in order to achieve our ultimate goal: getting our clients—the Kuwaiti detainees—some sort of due process so that they could prove their innocence and ultimately be released (or, obviously, if found guilty, receive their punishments). From the get-go, we knew that going to court, the first prong, was just one avenue for achieving that goal, and a slow one at that. We needed other avenues that would ultimately influence our government to change its policy at Guantánamo.

The second prong of our approach was diplomacy. We were fortunate that the Kuwaiti ambassador was willing to meet with us on a regular basis to discuss his citizens' predicament, provide what little information he had, and learn as much as he could from us about the legal case (and, eventually, about Guantánamo). Ambassador Salem Al-Sabah was direct and frank: The Kuwaiti government wanted its citizens back.

Sadly, it just wasn't that simple. Post–9/11, Kuwait, like many other countries, supported the U.S. in its quest to punish the perpetrators. Kuwait also relied on the U.S. for military protection, and the first Gulf War was a recent memory. The talks between Kuwait and the U.S. government, therefore, would be drawn out over the next several years, with the Kuwait government subtly pressuring the U.S. to release its citizens back to the custody of Kuwait, where they would be properly investigated and face trial if necessary under Kuwait law. Despite the friendly relations between the two countries, the U.S. proved stubborn, and it would be years before the Kuwaiti citizens would be sent home.

The third prong of our strategy, we soon came to realize, would have to be played out in the court of public opinion. We needed to generate public awareness of the situation at Guantánamo—that prisoners were being held incommunicado without any rights at all. Once the public learned the truth, we hoped they would pressure the government to do the right thing. So while we were preparing our complaint and responding to the government's motion to dismiss, we were also reaching out to the media to try to get our clients' side of the story in the papers.

Before any lawyers entered the picture, most news articles depicted all of the Guantánamo detainees as being "the worst of the worst," undeserving of any rights—hardened terrorists who'd been picked up on the battlefield, ready to kill American women and children given the chance. This made it hard to get anyone interested in hearing about our cause. John Mintz of *The Washington Post* was one of the few journalists willing to even meet with us. He relayed that the media was getting blacklisted at White House press conferences if they pressed too hard, or asked difficult questions. The truth was, at that time there were many different individuals at Guantánamo— more than six hundred men from forty-two countries. Many of them were not picked up on the "battlefield"; some of them had been turned over for bounties, paid by the U.S.; and, most significantly, not a single one had been given a hearing or trial in which they'd been found guilty of being terrorists, or even enemy combatants.

In July of 2002, we got a lucky break. Roy Gutman, who had won the Pulitzer Prize for his reporting in Bosnia, published an article in *Newsweek* after sending investigators to Kuwait, Pakistan, and Afghanistan. The investigators had determined that many of the Kuwaitis who were being held at Guantánamo had been kidnapped by tribesmen and turned over to Pakistani authorities—for *money*. The chain of custody (and the motive for calling someone a terrorist) was starting to look very suspicious.

Asked whether our clients were innocent or guilty, Tom used to say in interviews, "If they are guilty, hang them up by their toes—but there should be some process to determine who is a real combatant and who is an innocent civilian, picked up by mistake." (Actually, in the privacy of his office, Tom used to say that if any of the detainees were guilty, they should be "strung up by their balls," but I suspect his good judgment kept him from saying that on camera.) Tom encouraged me to deal with the press. Always thinking of the best interests of his clients, he posed this question to the legal team and our public relations consultant, David Henderson: "Who do you think the viewers will stop and listen to—Kristine?" he asked, pointing at me, "Or me, a balding, white Jewish man?"

David just smiled. Tom was unlike a lot of partners at big firms; letting an associate do major press was unheard of, especially because most partners would have jumped at the chance to be in the spotlight. Tom's decisions were always based on what was best for the case, but he was also thoughtful about helping me advance in my career.

In January of 2003, we were approached by CNN to be interviewed by Wolf Blitzer, and we accepted without hesitation. But which one of us would do the interview? It was up to Tom, who looked at me and said, "I know you can do it, kid." David helped me train for my first television interview; although I had already done BBC radio, this was big-time.

"Quit looking to God for help, Kristine," David gently suggested when I nervously glanced up and around during our practice sessions. We all went to the studio together, Tom and David as my entourage. While getting my makeup done by a

CNN makeup artist, memories of modeling came flooding back to me. But, oh this was so vastly different. My stomach was queasy, and I had to run to the bathroom three times to pee and check my lipstick before they called for me. Wolf perfunctorily introduced himself, while the techies adjusted my mic and earpiece. Everything was going just fine until he whipped out a piece of paper and said, "Kristine, I want to read to you and our viewers, a statement the Pentagon has put out, and then get your specifics on this case, as well as some information about the other six hundred detainees." *Oh Jesus*, I thought. *What is about to come out of his mouth? What is the Pentagon going to say? More importantly, what am I going to say in response?*

"The Pentagon says this: 'These individuals, the detainees, are enemy combatants captured in connection with an ongoing armed conflict. They continue to be enemy combatants,'" Wolf said, reading from the statement. He went on a little longer, giving me time to think, thank God, and then asked, "Why do you disagree with the Pentagon's assessment of these detainees?"

"Well, *calling* them 'enemy combatants' doesn't make it so," I said, practically pouting—but I rallied to clarify my point with a carefully articulated comeback. Tom would later refer to this as the "Saying It Doesn't Make It So" argument. I had challenged the government on broadcast television, which, after hearing the stories from the journalists we'd been working with, I knew to be a risky proposition. But I would be vindicated five years later, when the D.C. Circuit Court wrote in response to the government's accusations of a Guantánamo detainee:

"[T]he fact that the government has 'said it thrice' does not make an allegation true." They had cited Lewis Carroll, author of *Alice in Wonderland*.

Composing another letter to my mom (*Dear Mom: You won't believe who I was just being interviewed by . . .*), I rushed straight from the CNN interview to the airport. I was flying to New Orleans to attend the wedding of Elaine and Josh, good friends of mine. I would be meeting my new boyfriend at the airport—it was our first trip together. We had met a few months earlier at a black-tie gala at the Smithsonian Museum of Natural History; he was looking very smart in a tux, hovering over the buffet table, and looking a little like an Italian John F. Kennedy Jr. Of course I approached him! It didn't take more than one or two dates to learn that Bryan Di Lella was a Republican—a very devoted Republican, loyal to President Bush.

We hadn't really discussed politics or my work too much, dancing around the fact that we were likely to strongly disagree with each other on the administration's policy in the "war on terror." Bryan was not one to make quick judgments; he listened, observed, and more often than not, he was quite reserved. But it was one thing to disagree in private, and quite another for your girlfriend to go on national TV and tell the whole world she thought the administration was breaking the law. I was very proud of my CNN interview, but wondered what Bryan was going to say about it. Had he even watched the interview? Was he going to break up with me? Refuse to go on the trip with me? It turned out that Bryan had actually left work in the middle of the day to get to a TV with cable so he could watch my interview. Though he didn't comment on the substance of my words, he was clearly impressed and proud of me, and didn't hesitate to tell me so. Phew. Everything was going to work out.

Back in D.C., after the lower court dismissed our cases, we—as did the lawyers representing the two British citizens and the two Australian citizens also being held at Guantánamo—appealed the decision to the next level, the D.C. Circuit Court. The two teams were allowed to file their own briefs, but there would be one panel of three judges reviewing the cases and hearing oral arguments, which ultimately forced us all to work together. By mid-2003, our arguments had become more sophisticated, and we had made some inroads with the media, which was beginning to report more and more on Guantánamo, and with a tone slightly more critical of the administration than before.

However, we didn't have too much hope that the D.C. Circuit Court panel we had drawn would be sympathetic, as two out of three were notoriously conservative. The odds weren't good, and as we expected, the D.C. Circuit bought the government's theory and affirmed the dismissal of the case. We only had one more chance: the Supreme Court. Toward the end of 2003, we filed a petition for a writ of certiorari with the highest court in the land, and crossed our fingers. Less than 10 percent of the cases seeking review are granted the famous writ and given a chance to go before the nine justices.

We were a bit surprised and quite relieved when the Court decided to hear our case. Many people had considered our chances slim, but we hoped the fact that they were willing to hear us out meant that they at least partially disagreed with the decisions we'd received from the lower courts, and wanted to change the outcome. After the Court agreed to hear the case, we filed more briefs to fully explain why the U.S. courts should have jurisdiction over the claims of the Guantánamo detainees challenging their detention. These "merits briefs" were filed in December 2003 and January 2004, nearly three years after the first detainees were brought to Guantánamo. The next step was to tackle the difficult task of preparing for the oral argument, which would be held in a few months.

Putting together and preparing for an oral argument in front of the Supreme Court is no easy task—particularly when you're working with more than one team of lawyers, all of whom have ideas about how the case should be presented, what parts of the law to emphasize, what terminology should be used, what details to cite, and who would be best to present the case. At the Supreme Court level, it's common practice for law firms to hire an attorney with Supreme Court experience to present their case for them. It's a grand stage, and even many of the most experienced partners at big law firms have never had a chance to present an oral argument in front of the Supreme Court. As we were taking on the government and there appeared to be no end in sight to the "global war on terror," we needed to exercise extreme consideration before choosing who we wanted to argue the case on our behalf.

We'd been working with a few professors, including well-known Tony Amsterdam of New York University Law School, the father of clinical education. (He is also famous for his handlebar mustache, but that's another story.) Amsterdam had argued before the Supreme Court numerous times, and initially, Tom had wanted him to present our case for us. When we approached Tony about it, however, he made a wise point: "You know," he said, "for this case, I don't think I'm the best person for the job. The justices, they know me, and they know I'm really liberal. That's not the voice you want."

I was just beginning to learn how much work goes into a Supreme Court oral argument—and the law was just the half of it. Everything else was about presentation, who was delivering the message, how it was being delivered, and which of the justices you were trying to convince. Who was on the edge— Kennedy? O'Connor?

We all liked Tony, but agreed that while he was undeniably capable and could probably persuade a priest to smoke crack, he was a raving liberal, and everybody knew it. A second option, Michael Ratner, head of CCR, was smart and savvy, but we feared he was also too liberal for appearances' sake. And while Tom and Joe Margulies were both capable, both wanted to do the argument and we agreed that we should not split our collective time between two lawyers. We were going to have to find somebody that we could all agree on, and who had the right experience and ability to present our case effectively. We needed somebody who was a brilliant orator and had moral authority. We chose John Gibbons.

John had been appointed by President Reagan to the Court of Appeals for the Third Circuit, eventually becoming Chief Justice. He was a Republican-appointed Republican, who had sat on the bench, had taught constitutional law at Seton Hall Law School, and now practiced law at his own firm. It seemed like the perfect choice: He had great experience, he was very much on our side with respect to the detainees at Guantánamo, and he had the credibility we needed in order the keep the justices from seeing us as a group of bleeding-heart liberals.

Once our decision had been made, we spent every waking moment over the next couple of months preparing John for oral argument, a process that consisted of hour after hour in meetings with John, walking through every single question we could think of that the justices might ask, grilling him on the law, playing devil's advocate, pretending to be the government, and coming up with hypotheticals and extreme scenarios. How would he answer it all? We considered which points we might concede if pressed; we strategized, and practiced as if we were helping John rehearse for a starring role in a Hollywood movie.

For me, it was amazing. There I was, a sixth-year associate, assisting a former chief justice of a federal circuit court, alongside famous professors, to prepare for an oral argument in a highly controversial case that was being watched by the entire country—the entire world—and I was a part of it all. A few short years before, I had been a noodle-eating, hardly sleeping, posing-for-pictures student at Columbia University. My life had changed dramatically in a short period of time. I couldn't have been happier.

When our court date arrived, every one of us felt we knew the ins and outs of our argument, backwards and forwards, upside-down and sideways; we just hoped John did, too. John Gibbons, Tom Wilner, and Joe Margulies sat at the counsels' table. The remaining members of the two legal teams had special seating in the courtroom, since we were "on the briefs" (part of the legal team that was representing a party). Again, I couldn't believe this was all really happening. It was my first time even being inside the Supreme Court, and I was actually part of the legal team presenting an argument before the justices. In law school, I had only read about them—Scalia, Stevens, O'Connor, Rehnquist—and these kinds of cases. These were the cases that made history, and there I was, living it!

The argument seemed to go well, but the justices weren't interested in making anyone feel comfortable. John was "one of them," so to speak, but they didn't exactly give him a pass; who knows what would have happened if he had been somebody else? It was fascinating for me to see the way the nine justices approached an oral argument. Before that day, the only justice I'd ever heard speak was Ruth Bader Ginsburg. She's amazing, but I'd never seen the others in action. I was surprised by the fact that they had no qualms about showing the lawyers which way they were determined to vote; it was as if they had already made up their minds and they either wanted confirmation or divine intervention. Justice Scalia, the ultimate conservative, grilled John a bit about his arguments. Then Justice Breyer, a much less conservative justice, would throw a softball question at John as a way of responding to Scalia's original question. Although Scalia would snap a retort back to John, it was clear that Scalia and Breyer were using John as a way to debate with each other.

Ted Olson, as the solicitor general, made the argument on behalf of the government. His wife, Barbara, had been on the plane that crashed into the Pentagon. As he started out his argument, briefly reminding the justices of the terrible terrorist acts of 9/11, I was sure they wouldn't ask him any tough questions. But, the nine justices didn't hold back; I found myself believing that justice would be served.

After our time was up and the next case called, we walked away, thinking that all of the time we'd spent working on this litigation—talking about it, writing about it, debating it—had come to an end. With the conclusion of oral arguments, we were finished; there was nothing more to do. Now we had to wait until the Court issued its opinion. It could take a month, a few months, or even a year, if the individual justices couldn't make up their minds or felt the need to have their clerks do additional research.

The Supreme Court's decision came out on June 29, 2004: The opinion reversed the earlier rulings, and held that federal courts *did* have the jurisdiction to hear the habeas petitions of prisoners at Guantánamo after all, according to a federal statute dictating that if you are in the custody of the United States, you can challenge your detention—regardless of where you are being held or who you are. Finally, after two and a half years of continuous litigation, we were starting to get somewhere. Our clients were going to have the opportunity to try to prove their innocence. And, we would get to meet them for the first time.

When a higher court makes a ruling, it often "remands" the case back to the lower court to execute the decision. Originally, we had gone to court challenging the way in which our clients were being detained—that is, without due process (or without legal counsel or a hearing, a mechanism to challenge their detention). But the government said that the courts didn't even have the authority to review that challenge. The Supreme Court's ruling in our consolidated case—titled *Rasul v. Bush*—said that the courts did have that authority, and, therefore, the detainees had the right to challenge their detentions in federal court. So basically, we had to go almost all the way back to square one, and get that right fulfilled: We had to go to court to challenge our clients' detentions.

The government's response to the new phase of the case was just as swift as it had been in the initial phase—an almost immediate motion to dismiss. The government claimed that while yes, detainees may have the right to *file* habeas petitions, and federal courts may have the authority to *hear* a habeas challenge, there were no underlying rights to be vindicated.

The detainees themselves, according to the government, had no constitutional rights. So while they could file petitions and the court could review them, the detainees were not entitled to "substantive due process" under the Fifth Amendment (which includes things such as the right not to be detained without a legal basis or a fair hearing)—and therefore, the courts should dismiss the case. If this doesn't make any sense, it's because it doesn't. The government was essentially claiming that the Supreme Court's decision in *Rasul* was nothing but a hollow guarantee.

Once the Supreme Court had confirmed that we had a right to bring a case on behalf of our clients, many other lawyers from big law firms decided it was now okay to pursue habeas petitions on behalf of detainees at Guantánamo. Some of these law firms were the same ones who had turned down the Kuwaiti families back in 2002 when it was too controversial to represent a detainee. CCR took on the administrative burden of coordinating the rapidly growing number of lawyers, and by the fall of 2004, there were thirteen detainee cases filed in the D.C. District Court.

Things started to get more complicated. Representing those thirteen cases, comprised of fifty or so detainees, was a group of about twenty-five to thirty lawyers. All had filed habeas petitions, and the government had filed the same motion to dismiss in every case, making the exact same argument. Instead of ruling on each motion individually, the district court decided to consolidate all the petitions under one judge and give the district court judges the opportunity to opt out. All of the judges save one opted for consolidation; thus, eleven cases were consolidated under Judge Green, while Judge Leon kept his two cases. Judge Leon was known to be very conservative, so things didn't look good for those lawyers who were before him.

Our case, *Al-Odah v. United States of America*, went into the first, larger group of cases under Judge Green, while Judge Leon's two cases included six detainees picked up in Bosnia, consolidated under the caption *Boumediene v. Bush*. Judge Leon agreed with the government and promptly dismissed his two cases. Judge Green, however, disagreed, deciding that the detainees had rights that had been violated under the Fifth Amendment:

> *No person shall be . . . compelled in any criminal case to be a witness against himself, nor be deprived of life, liberty, or property, without due process of law [emphasis added]; nor shall private property be taken for public use, without just compensation.*

In the meantime, while our cases were being consolidated and the government's motion to dismiss considered by the two district court judges, the Department of Defense (DOD) began holding military hearings called Combatant Status Review Tribunals (CSRTs). Just two weeks after the *Rasul* decision held that the detainees did have the statutory right to habeas, the government issued DOD regulations establishing the procedures for these CSRTs. The government continued to insist that the detainees did not have constitutional rights and should not be in federal court. By holding these military hearings, the administration was hoping that if a court found the detainees actually *did* have constitutional rights, those rights would be satisfied by the CSRTs.

Luckily for us (and for our clients, whom we still hadn't met), Judge Green disagreed. In her opinion, the detainees *did* have Fifth Amendment rights, and the military CSRT hearings provided to the detainees by DOD weren't in keeping with those rights. The CSRT procedures, in fact, did not look anything like our own criminal justice system, or even any of the military hearings held in past wars. With a CSRT, the detainee was not allowed to have a lawyer; secret evidence could be used against him; evidence obtained through torture could be used against him; and the executive branch (the President or DOD), not some impartial court or tribunal, had the final say. As a result, the individual could be detained and cut off from his family and the world, in virtual isolation, for the rest of his life. The CSRT procedures would continue to be the subject of heated debate between military lawyers, constitutional and international law scholars, criminal defense lawyers, and the government, and whether they were fair would be the primary subject of the ongoing litigation for the next four long years.

The situation was a conundrum, not entirely atypical of our justice system: Two different judges on the same court addressing the same legal arguments came out with two different decisions. Not surprisingly, the government appealed Judge Green's decision, while the lawyers representing the detainees under

Judge Leon appealed his decision, as well. After the Supreme Court ruled in our favor, followed by Judge Green's decision— again, in our favor—I was hopeful that our clients would finally see the inside of a courtroom. The appeals made it clear we were in for a long haul.

Despite the difficulties, I found myself just soaking it all in. This case taught me a great deal about everything involved in my profession: the chain of litigation, being before the highest court in the land, advocacy and diplomacy, and working with the media. I wasn't just learning about it; I was living it. The appeals moved both cases up the chain, to the Court of Appeals for the D.C. Circuit Court, the middle appellate court, at which point both cases were consolidated and referred to as *Al-Odah v. United States*, even though it included the *Boumediene* case as well.

This presented yet another lawyerly challenge—how to get thirteen legal teams, the majority of which were large law firms (full of partners with lots of experience and the egos to go with it), to work together on such a complex and controversial case. Although consolidated, the Green petitioners and the Leon petitioners were each allowed to submit their own sets of briefs. There were eleven legal teams in the Green group, and we only had the opportunity to submit two briefs— an opening brief and a reply brief—so it really had to be a true collaboration.

As the only firm involved in the litigation since day one, our team at Shearman became the lead drafters of the briefs, often getting the final say after hours—no, days—of debate. CCR's Michael Ratner and others had been involved just as long, but they had limited resources and were happy to have someone else take the lead. In short, it was a logistical nightmare. Every time a draft was completed and circulated to the various teams, it would be returned with no less than eleven sets of comments—some conflicting, some we disagreed with, some that were helpful. We would then spend hours upon hours in conference calls, dissecting the legal arguments, the comments, and the reasoning, attempting to work it all out. Our working relationships were often fraught with personality clashes, short tempers, and infighting. Tom was not exactly a wilting flower, nor were some of the other lawyers involved. I often found myself the mediator between some very strong wills. The whole process was an amazing opportunity for me to learn firsthand about different lawyering styles and varied approaches to legal analysis and substantive legal theories. Differences here are not a disadvantage; in fact, they are necessary if you want to develop the strongest legal argument and strategy.

At the same time we were arguing over constitutional law and cases from World War II, we were also fighting for the right to see our clients—at Guantánamo. We had been representing them for over two and half years and still hadn't been allowed any face-to-face contact with them. Since the government controlled the military base, the only thing we could do was fight it out in court. The Supreme Court had said we could challenge our clients' detentions, but how could we do that effectively if we couldn't meet with them?

By this point, the court was putting sufficient pressure on the government for it to concede that the detainees would be allowed to have lawyers—although initially it had maintained that just because they were allowed to file habeas petitions didn't mean they were entitled to counsel. The government still held the position that every aspect of our communication with the detainees would need to be monitored out of concern for national security. They wanted to hear our conversations with clients and read the mail we sent to them, along with the notes from our client meetings—even though all of this was an outrageous violation of attorney-client privilege. We refused, and more briefs were filed debating what restraints were appropriate in this situation. We submitted a moderate proposal to the court, one that maintained attorney-client confidentiality but still protected national security.

Eventually, we won; the judge agreed that some rules should be imposed regarding how we would communicate with our clients, but the government would not be allowed carte blanche when it came to all of our communications and notes. There had to be *some* protection of attorney-client confidentiality. The court ultimately issued a "protective order," which dictated that all of the information we gained from our clients was presumptively classified. In order to share it with anyone other than the court or our team—the families and the public—we would have to get it declassified by submitting the information to a "privilege team" who would review it for classified information.

With the terms finally stipulated by the court, there was no time to lose: It was December of 2004, and we were going to make our first trip to Guantánamo.

11

Guantánamo 24/7

Preparing for our first trip to Guantánamo was like preparing for the first trip to the moon. We didn't know what to expect. Before any of the detainees' lawyers were allowed to visit the detainees, the only nongovernmental employees who'd been able to access the detention center—aside from the International Committee for the Red Cross (ICRC)—had been a small group of journalists, and they were not allowed to talk to the detainees. That's where the first images of Camp X-Ray came from: pictures of detainees on their knees wearing orange jumpsuits, blacked-out goggles, and earmuffs, with soldiers in the background. It was a harsh image and the world's first glimpse of Gitmo.

That picture and a few others provided our only glimpse of what life at Gitmo might be like for our clients. We knew they'd originally been kept outdoors in makeshift cells, with corrugated tin roofs and chain-link fences for walls, open to the elements. If it rained, they got wet. If it was hot and sunny, they got sunburned. Their "facilities" were as simple as a bucket for a toilet. When we finally got to meet our clients, we found out that this wasn't the worst of it: They were eaten alive by insects, harassed by banana rats, and kept in their cells for nearly twenty-four hours at a time, without access to any kind of reading material other than the Koran (and even that was not provided for a few months), and not allowed prayer time or exercise. After almost five months at Camp X-Ray, they were transferred to the newly constructed detention camps, called Camp Delta, which included Camps One, Two, Three, and Four. Camp Five was constructed two years later, and Camp Six was completed in 2006.

Organizing a trip to Gitmo, particularly for the first time, is far from easy. It's not like booking a flight to anywhere else in the world; you can't just go to Expedia.com or use your frequent flyer miles. First, in order to actually visit the base and meet with your clients, you must get permission from the government—not only to get the appropriate clearances, but also simply to coordinate the actual dates that you'd like to meet with your clients at Gitmo, which you must submit at least three weeks in advance. The government can always turn you down, saying the dates don't work due to "camp operations," or some other unspecified reason. After the dates are approved, you must contact one of only two independent air carriers that fly to Guantánamo—Air Sunshine or Lynx Air. And these are not commercial jets; they are ten- to fourteen-seater commuter planes that fly back and forth only once a day, and not even every day. Getting a reservation on those flights was like getting into a trendy club in New York, only harder. On our first trip, it was just Neil Koslowe and me. We left the day after Christmas, 2004.

We had no idea how we'd be received by our clients, if they'd trust us, or if they'd be willing to speak to us at all. As a gesture of our good intentions, we'd decided to bring some specialty foods for them, since we had no idea what they'd been eating for the past two years. We brought boxes of baklava from a pastry shop in Detroit that we knew made really great, authentic baklava. The brother of our legal assistant—Uzma Rasool—drove to the store himself and shipped it to us by FedEx. We had also asked Khalid Al-Odah, the father of one of our clients and the families' representative, to work with the other families to put together a DVD, as a way to show our clients (whom we'd never met) that we really were who we said we were—their lawyers—and not some spies for the CIA who were just trying to get more information out of them. (Being mistaken for a government spy is, for some reason, a recurring theme in my life.) In addition to bringing along the DVD, we asked the families to write letters to their sons, as extra insurance in the event that the government wouldn't allow us to play the DVD for our clients.

After the initial arrival, which consisted of a search of our luggage, presentation of our clearances, and having pictures taken for our badges, we arrived at the Combined Bachelor Quarters (CBQ), our accommodations, around seven o'clock—after the cafeteria had closed for the night. We scrounged up what little food we could, mostly what we'd brought with us, and called it a night. We were travel-weary, pensive, and unsure of what we would face the next day. What would our clients be like? What would they look like? Would they be aggressive terrorists who could "chew through hydraulic cable" to kill

Americans, like General Myers had once said during a news broadcast back in 2002? Would they be happy to see us? We didn't know.

The next morning, we met our translator, "AM," got on the school bus that was making its rounds of the Leeward Side of the base, and boarded the ferry to get to the Windward Side of the base, where the detention camp was located. Our military escort met us at the ferry landing. Yet again, I hadn't known what to pack, and ended up selecting my same trusty, loose suit, conservative shoes, and a head scarf, just in case (which AM suggested wasn't necessary). As it turned out, there was no end to the suggestions AM would make during our visits to Guantánamo. He was our translator, our "cultural broker," our negotiator when communications with our military escort broke down, our friend, and a friend to the detainees. We would use him on every trip and he never turned us down, even referring to us as the "Gitmo Dream Team" on several occasions.

"I don't think you need a head scarf, Kristine," he said. "That might be a little too much. I think they'll think you're trying to be someone you're not. They've met American women before. Some of the guards are females."

"You don't think they'll see it as a gesture of respect? Are you sure?" I asked warily. I wasn't quite ready to trust AM's cultural knowledge. "Does Gita wear a scarf?" Gita Gutierrez had worked with John Gibbons and now worked for CCR; she had been to the base once already, and I knew she was smart. I trusted her judgment.

"No, she doesn't. I think you'll be fine without one. You're dressed very conservatively," AM said, wrinkling his nose at my baggy, wrinkled suit. I could sense that AM was appreciative of the gesture even if he didn't think it was necessary, and I supposed he was right; after all, we were (sort of) in U.S. territory.

"Okay, I trust you," I said, even though I wasn't sure I did. Nevertheless, I was willing to try. For the time being, AM was our only conduit to our clients.

Those first meetings with our clients at Guantánamo—in which we played the DVD from their families, introduced ourselves to them, and began the long process of getting to know them—were epic moments in my legal career . . . in my life. It was unlike any other client meeting I'd ever had. (Indeed, the last time I'd met with a client, I had been sitting at the bar of the Four Seasons in New York.) Neil, Tom, and I had spent more than two years of our lives working on behalf of these men that we'd never met, and it felt strange to know *of* them but not to know them.

We were brought into an interview room at Camp Echo where we found one of our clients sitting at a small card table, handcuffed and chained to an O-ring bolted to the floor. Suddenly, seeing a real person in front of me, I realized that until that moment, I'd thought of our clients as a faceless group— "The Twelve Kuwaitis"—like some forgotten religious order (and they *were* forgotten, in a way). Sometimes I even thought of my client as being the "Rule of Law," as that was often how I tried to explain my work to the press and other audiences. After meeting them, though, and putting faces with names, I'd never be able to think of them that way again. They were people, too, and even though I'd known it all along, it had become a distant fact after months filled with litigation, when any rare time to myself had been filled with enjoying my American freedoms. Meanwhile, these men, my clients, were being held as criminals, accused of nothing and yet certainly suspected of much.

Over the course of three or four days, Neil and I spent about three hours with each client. We introduced ourselves, offered them some baklava (discovering that what they really wanted was McDonald's or Pizza Hut), played the DVD, updated them on their families as a way of assuring them that we were in contact with them, and explained how we had become involved in their case. We asked them very few questions, as we felt they'd probably been asked enough questions for a lifetime by their interrogators. They had been through so much. We didn't want to initiate the attorney-client relationship with a pressured conversation. Our goal in those first meetings was simply to get them to trust us.

After that first day at Gitmo, a long day of meetings with the first few of our twelve clients, Neil and I were exhausted. Our military escort returned us to the ferry, which we took across the bay. We rode the school bus back to the CBQ, where we were staying, making the whole trip with barely a word spoken.

"It's evil in there," Neil said, breaking the silence. We'd both been so deep in thought I'd almost forgotten he was there.

"I know," I said. "I think I need a shower. It might make me feel better."

"Me too," Neil responded. "And then I'm going to turn on the TV and find out what has been going on in the rest of the world."

The news wasn't good. We'd arrived at Guantánamo on December 26, 2004, but had been too exhausted from travel to bother turning on the TV. We'd gotten up so early on the next day that it was only now, on the evening of the twenty-seventh, that we got news of the terrible tsunami that had hit South Asia, where I'd traveled only a few years before. To be at Gitmo, meeting men who had been held (but never charged) by our government in such harsh conditions, and then to learn about such a horrific event in another part of the world . . . It further cemented our dark moods. I was overwhelmed with many emotions. The world seemed full of tragedy, and as I watched the news of the devastation, tears streamed down my face.

The next morning, we got back to work. The detainees seemed to have a hard time believing we were real. After two years with no contact that wasn't an interrogation or confrontational in some way, we must have seemed like a mirage. One client, in fact, suggested that we were actors in a grand play the military was producing. As we parted they'd ask us if we'd be back tomorrow. Could we bring them a Diet Coke—or maybe a pizza? Anything they asked, we tried to do. We wanted them to trust us, to feel comfortable talking to us, to believe that we were there to try and help them. Some of the things they asked us for—mostly books and magazines—seemed harmless, but we weren't sure if we could get them for our clients, and that was hard to explain. After all, we'd just spent hours telling them about all of the great legal work we had done for them, and how global and reputable Shearman & Sterling was; how could we say that we couldn't get them a copy of *National Geographic*?

The DVD turned out to be our greatest asset. It began with a shot of the collected group of families in one room—actually, the men from the families, who we'd been working with all along, and several children, both boys and girls. Khalid was the spokesman, and explained what we'd already told our clients: how we got involved with the case, what we'd been working on for the past two years, and why it had taken us so long to be able to visit them. Khalid then emphasized that we were their lawyers, there to help them, and that they should trust us. Each family member said hello, even the children. We knew the DVD would have an impact on our clients, but we had no idea to what extent. It turned out that the detainees at Gitmo had created a strong network and were able to pass along information effectively and swiftly. Word eventually spread throughout the camp that *our* clients had been able to watch a DVD of their families. It became apparent that none of the other legal teams had thought of making DVDs to bring with them, and apparently this was a matter of contention between some of the other detainees and their attorneys.

Every detainee had questions about his family. One asked about his son's heart operation, which had been scheduled for two weeks after the return date of his trip to Iran, where he'd been picked up by the U.S. Another, Abdullah, a former professional soccer player, had left his pregnant wife behind when he'd gone on a trip that was only supposed to last ten days. We told him that he had a new daughter, and that she and her mother were doing well. Although he'd gotten word from his family (through heavily censored and redacted mail) that he had a new baby girl, he was never sure if he could trust the letters, which clearly had been read and heavily handled by his captors. Having someone on his side tell him in person that he had a daughter who was doing well brought a huge sparkle of joy to Abdullah's eyes, in stark contrast to his handcuffs, his bare cell, and his prison jumpsuit.

Even if some of the detainees didn't want to listen to us talk about their legal case, all of them were glad to hear their families were doing well. Slowly, as we began to gain their trust, they began telling us of their treatment in the custody of the U.S.—first in Bagram or Kandahar, and then at Guantánamo. They'd been beaten on several occasions, and forced to sleep on the ground. They confirmed that in the very early days, they hadn't been allowed prayer time (and when they were, the guards disrupted the call to prayer); that they weren't given a Koran to read for the first several months, and they had no other reading materials; they were not allowed to socialize with or even see other detainees, nor were they given much if any time to exercise. Mail from their families was withheld for unusually long periods of time. Some of them had spent more than a month in isolation, and all of them spent at least twenty-three hours a day in their cells, taking all of their meals there, and with bright lights on twenty-four hours a day, seven days a week. They all reported that their medical attention had been inadequate, and that they hadn't seen a dentist during their two and half years at Gitmo, which was one of the first things we reported in the press. Happily, the next time we visited, Abdullah reported that he'd been visited by a dentist. He was thrilled. Every little thing we could do to improve our clients' lives while they were at Gitmo brought us a little more trust, a little more clout.

Returning to D.C. after that first trip to Guantánamo was a relief. Neil and I explained our entire trip in detail to Tom. Prior to leaving Guantánamo, we had organized our notes, and pursuant to the protective order gave them to our military escort in a sealed envelope with our initials over the seal. He sent the envelope via a secure channel back to a "secure facility" in northern Virginia—a physical location that houses classified information and which is "secure" (in other words, its walls, floors, and ceilings are specially reinforced and routinely swept for bugs). Any notes taken from our meetings with clients were presumptively classified, and, as the court had ordered, if we wanted to share that information with anyone other than the court and each other (we had all gotten "secret" clearance), we had to submit it to the government's "privilege team," made up of court security officers who were employed by the Department of Justice (DOJ).

The court required a "Chinese wall" (essentially an information barrier) between the DOJ privilege team and the DOJ lawyers who were our opposing counsel in the ongoing litigation, to ensure that no attorney-client privileged information would be disclosed or leaked to the lawyers representing the government. The privilege team would review the notes and determine which information could be declassified, and which information had to remain classified, to ensure that any sensitive information—anything that could jeopardize national security—did not get disclosed to the public. Though I understood such precautions were to protect national security, it was still frustrating to us and to the families of our clients that we had to wait several days after our return to reveal what we'd learned. We weren't allowed to speak to anyone without security clearance about what we'd learned from out clients until our notes had been cleared—and then, we could only reveal the information that had been declassified. Luckily at that time, there were still only a small number of lawyers traveling to Guantánamo, so it was only a few days before our notes were declassified and we could call the Kuwaiti families to tell them about their sons.

"Good afternoon, everyone," Tom said to begin the meeting. We had set up a conference call with the Shearman team on one end, and the Kuwaiti families on the other. "As you know, Neil and Kristine have just returned from Guantánamo. We could not call you immediately because we must follow the court's order and submit our notes first for declassification.

Overall, the visit went well, and the team was able to visit with all of the Kuwaiti citizens. To begin with, here's where we stand: Most of your sons agreed to sign the forms allowing us to continue to represent them, so for that reason alone, our first trip to Guantánamo was fairly productive."

Neil was nodding his head in agreement and getting ready to pick up where Tom left off, but I couldn't take it any longer—I interjected.

"Listen," I said. "What you all probably want to know right away is whether or not your sons are okay. We met with each Kuwaiti citizen. Physically, they are . . . fine. They have been through a lot, but they are alive. They have no disabling injuries; they have, um, their arms, their legs, and their bodies intact." I glanced over at Tom, who was nodding at me. I couldn't lie to our clients' families and say their sons were perfectly fine or in great shape, but I didn't want to scare them, either.

"Kristine is right," he said. "We should've started by saying that your sons are all in decent health, considering the circumstances. They very much enjoyed watching the DVD you made, and we think that made a big difference in their willingness to speak with us. Your sons were all very eager for news of their families, and were glad to hear that you are all well." He paused, looking at me for a moment before continuing. "Now, let's get back to the next course of action . . ."

For me, hearing the families' sighs of relief and joy at finally knowing for sure that their sons were alive and relatively healthy—prisoners or not—was the reward for all of the hard work, all of the late nights, all of the brief-writing, and even the hate e-mails and nasty comments that we had received over the past two and a half years. Once again, I was learning what it really meant to be a lawyer. Something that Michael Ratner, president of CCR and a human rights, fight-the-power super-hero, had said once came to mind: "Lawyers bring light to dark places." He was right: That was exactly what we were trying to do at Guantánamo. Michael's phrase would keep me going during the dark times when I felt our work was completely useless, or worse, unpatriotic and anti-American.

That first visit was only the beginning. For the next year, Neil, Tom, and I would travel to Gitmo an average of once every three or four weeks. Sometimes all three of us would go, sometimes just two of us. There were other people on the Shearman Kuwaiti team who also went to Gitmo over the next year: Jared Goldstein (attorney), Uzma Rasool (legal assistant), and Amanda Shafer (attorney). It was not an easy trip, and after several months of visiting Guantánamo numerous times, I was relieved when someone else other than me would make the trip, even though I felt guilty for not personally going to see my clients. When we'd return, the routine was always the same: We'd submit our notes to the privilege team, and once they were cleared, we would tell the families of our visit and speak to the press.

In early 2005, ours was one of the few legal teams regularly traveling to Guantánamo, and now that the media had picked up on the story in a bigger way, speaking to us was the only avenue for the press—and the public—to hear what the detainees were saying. Though the press had been allowed to travel to the base, journalists had never been allowed to talk to the detainees, nor had any other outside entity other than the ICRC. We were a conduit to the prisoners at one of the world's most infamous prisons.

After the notes from our first visit were cleared, and we'd spoken with the families, we hosted a press conference for Middle Eastern media outlets to inform them of the situation at Guantánamo as told to us by our clients. The legal team (Tom, Neil, and I) and David, our PR guy, had once again decided that I would be the best spokesperson for our clients. I didn't hold back. I explained how the detainees' right to religion was being discriminated against; one of our clients had told me that the Koran was being mistreated at Guantánamo. It had been thrown in the toilet, stomped on, and mishandled. (Months later, *Newsweek* would come out with a story from a different source that the Koran had been thrown in the toilet, causing riots across the globe, but they later retracted the story under pressure. I had learned the truth before it ever became national news, and I wasn't afraid to tell the press what I knew.)

I also reported the other mistreatments and inhumane conditions: no other reading materials; very little exercise; twenty-three hours a day in their cells, which were brightly lit and under- or overheated; inadequate medical treatment. One detainee had suffered a broken arm when an Immediate Reaction Force (IRF) team had gotten a little too rough with him.

The response from the public was less than sympathetic. Most people would say, "Well, they're not being tortured, are they? We aren't pulling out their fingernails, are we?" In my mind, being forced to sit in a freezing-cold cell, alone, for twenty-three hours a day, without reading materials or exercise, with the lights on day and night, without any physical contact with family, all for more than two years straight, *is* a form of torture, particularly when you've had no trial or been convicted of anything!

Beyond that, I felt that the work I was doing was important. Innocent or guilty, my clients had a right to some sort of fair hearing, and that's what I was fighting for. We weren't asking the government to release its detainees; we were simply asking that they be allowed to try to prove that they weren't enemy combatants. If the government thought they had committed some crime, then they should be charged and brought to trial, just as any other criminal would in our country—or any civilized country, for that matter.

The U.S. government, for its part, had held hearings of some sort—military CSRT hearings. Unfortunately, however, they were a farce, often described as "Kafkaesque" for their absurdity, and a major reason our case had been allowed to proceed by Judge Green in the first place. The military CSRT hearings were established two weeks after the *Rasul* decision, clearly as an attempt to avoid the import of court's ruling (that the detainees were entitled to hearings in *federal* court), and were held to determine whether the detainees' status as "enemy combatants" should continue. They have been sharply criticized by attorneys, academics, JAGs ("judge advocate generals," or military lawyers), judges, NGOs, Congress, and most recently, the Supreme Court, because of their abject unfairness, even for suspected terrorists. Two and half years after they had been picked up and held incommunicado, the detainees were allowed to participate in these hearings to try to prove that they weren't who the government thought they were.

But the CSRT hearings had some serious defects: The detainees were not allowed to have an attorney; in many cases, they were told about their upcoming hearing just a week before it was held; secret evidence was used against them; hearsay evidence and evidence obtained through torture was used against them; government evidence was presumptively reliable and accurate; in all cases a request for a witness was denied; in most cases a detainee's request for documentary evidence was denied; the ultimate appeal was to the executive; and the burden was on the detainee to prove that he wasn't an enemy combatant.

In some cases, it turned out that the CSRT panel determined that the detainee was a non–enemy combatant (NEC) or "no longer an enemy combatant" (NLEC), but the panel was asked by its superiors to hold another hearing, review their decision, and come to a different one (the government refused to admit that they may have picked up the wrong person). One of my clients was accused of being an enemy combatant because he wore a Casio watch, had traveled to Afghanistan with money, and his alias had been found on the hard drive of a computer in the safe house of an alleged al-Qaeda member.

When asked to respond to this latter charge, the hearing went something like this:

"I have no alias . . . What is the alias that I am accused of having?" asked my client.

"We can't tell you; it's classified information," responded the tribunal.

"Well, where is the safe house located, where the computer with my alias was found?" my client asked.

"It's classified."

"What about the name of the alleged al-Qaeda member?"

"It's classified."

"How am I supposed to defend myself?"

How *was* he supposed to defend himself or answer the allegations against him? The CSRTs were, simply put, a sham, or as Neil described them, "kangaroo courts." This was not justice.

I became a pretty frequent visitor to Guantánamo in the next few months. We felt that with the pressure we were putting on the government in court, along with the growing interest in our case from the media and the general public, the tide was slowly starting to turn—at least a little bit. More and more information was coming out in the media about the conditions at Guantánamo. Former detainees were speaking out and telling the world that they had been abused and tortured, and more lawyers from notable law firms were willing to represent detainees.

Less than three months after our first visit, we filed a big motion called a "preliminary injunction." An injunction essentially stops the offending party—in this case, the government—from continuing its behavior, or it forces the offending party to change its behavior. Our injunction included affidavits from the detainees, some of them handwritten, in an attempt to get better living conditions for our clients. If they were going to be detained "until the end of hostilities," as the government used to say to justify the detentions without charges, we thought the government should at least provide conditions that were humane and not for the sole purpose of punishing detainees who hadn't even been proven guilty.

The government was good at talking out of both sides of its mouth. On the one hand, the detainees were not charged because they were merely being detained until the end of the war, but on the other hand, they were treated harshly because they were considered terrorists, unlawful enemy combatants. So the detainees were in limbo, treated like criminals but charged with no crimes "for the duration of the hostilities." In our motion, we again described their current lives: The lack of reading materials and exercise, the isolation, the extremely bright lights focused on their cells for twenty-four hours a day (making it very difficult for them to sleep), their struggles to deal with freezing temperatures (often without blankets) or extremely hot temperatures (with no air conditioning, or even fans to help circulate air), the inadequate medical and dental care (specifically, that they had been given medications surreptitiously in their water without being told what they were receiving).

We then filed a motion to request that our clients be given English-Arabic dictionaries so that they could understand the legal materials we sent in the mail and brought on every visit; they wanted to be able to communicate with us more effectively and without having to rely on a translator all the time. That request didn't fly with the government at all; they responded that an English-Arabic dictionary could not be given to the detainees because they would "create dangers to national security and force protection at GTMO," specifically, that the detainees might be able to improve their English and "collect information against the United States by listening, for example, to guards, medical staff . . ."

Medical staff? To me, that was particularly troubling and revealing in regard to the government's policies when it came to enemy combatants at Guantánamo. *What exactly are the doctors and nurses doing or saying at Gitmo that the detainees shouldn't understand?* I wondered.

All of our motions were preceded by an initial request to the government, which summarily turned down every single one. The only option was to go to the court and ask for relief. It was during this period that I truly realized how much power a government can have over a person's life, and there is nothing a person can do about it other than use up time and resources, battling it out in court, where the solution, even if in your favor, could take months or years.

We also filed a motion with the court, after first getting turned down by the government, asking that we be allowed to provide each of our clients with a *tafsir*, which is a standard and scholarly commentary to the Koran. We even submitted an affidavit from the executive director of a well-known and respected American-Muslim group—the American Muslim Council—demonstrating that the *tafsir* is an apolitical, non-extremist educational tool for understanding the Koran. Like our other motions, the court didn't even bother to rule on it, and the government held fast to its refusal.

While we waited for the government to combat each motion we filed and the court to at least rule on the motions, we were battling obstacles, which the circumstances of Guantánamo had thrown into the attorney-client relationship, making it more difficult for our clients to trust us. While our clients were allowed to write to us, by the time their letters had gone through the proper channels and been delivered to us, we would have already returned to Guantánamo for our next visit. And when they would ask whether we'd brought them the things they'd requested or whether we'd looked into certain aspects of their case (things we didn't know they'd requested or asked about), we'd have to admit that we were empty-handed, or worse, look confused—not a great strategy for engendering continued faith in our abilities to help them.

That wasn't the worst of it; the government appeared to be doing everything it could to disrupt our relationships. We learned that an interrogator had said to two of our clients, "Your lawyers are Jews. Throughout history, Jews have betrayed Muslims. Don't you think your lawyers, who are Jews, will betray you?" Despite the fact that (obviously) we weren't going to "betray" our clients because they were Muslim (or for any other reason), and that by this point we had visited the detainees several times, it started to become more and more difficult to reassure them that we were on their side, that we were trying to help them. The interrogators' techniques were frustrating, to say the least. In an attempt to put a stop to that kind of behavior, Tom filed an affidavit detailing the interrogator's questions and insinuations. The court did nothing; it didn't even rule on our request. It was another lesson for me—that sometimes a lawyer is powerless, even when the law is on his or her side.

At the beginning, we thought things were going to get better, that our motions would be heard and the court would issue an order, maybe even in our favor, and that we'd be able to make improvements to our clients' lives for the duration of their detention at Guantánamo. After a while, though, it became clear that our judge didn't want to rule on our motions, that she was taking a wait-and-see attitude because the primary case was currently pending before the D.C. Circuit Court on the issue of whether or not the detainees could even challenge their detentions. Additionally, toward the end of 2005, it became clear that the conservative groups on the Hill were trying to get legislation passed that would overturn the *Rasul* decision, and that the detainees may have no right to be in court at all.

"They treat us like animals," Abdullah said during one visit in the summer of 2005.

I know, I thought. *It makes me feel sick to my stomach to think about it.* Many people I had come across never referred to the detainees as men who deserved basic human rights, but rather, as "terrorists" or "unlawful enemy combatants" who deserved nothing, as if these titles justified their dehumanization. Sometimes they were simply called "those people," a term referring not just to the Guantánamo detainees, but to all Muslims. Trying to remain positive, I asked, "What do you mean?"

"They don't look at us when they speak to us. They laugh at us when we ask for prayer time or the Koran," Abdullah continued. "They don't flinch when we cry out in pain."

The detainees' treatment was getting worse, and we couldn't do much about it. We provided the detainees' only nongovernmental account of the world, and we only saw our clients every few weeks, sometimes every six weeks—whereas the government had access to our clients twenty-four hours a day, and used that to its advantage.

In August, everything came to a head.

I was sitting in my office, staring out my window at the National Archives. *I should go visit again, take a look at the original Constitution*, thinking that we might not even have a Constitution in a few years if the Bush administration got its way. My phone rang and Neil's name popped up on caller ID.

"Can you swing by?" Neil asked, without the usual niceties. I walked the twenty-five feet to Neil's office, and Tom was there, sitting in one of the visitor chairs. I knew this was serious. *Let the powwow begin.*

"One of the habeas lawyers called Neil over the weekend," said Tom. "They were in Guantánamo and just got their notes cleared. One of their clients said there's a big hunger strike going on at Guantánamo, and that some of the Kuwaitis are participating." Tom almost never looked worried, but he did today.

"What?" I said, waiting for Tom's words to sink in. "Are you sure? Who? What can we do? How soon can we get down there?" I shot off a series of questions, then without waiting for a reply followed it with a pessimistic, "The court's not going to do anything, is it?" We were used to getting shot down. Shit, we were used to the court not lifting a finger even in the face of horrific accusations.

"Well, we don't have another visit planned right now," Tom said. "Neil's already called Andrew at DOJ; we're waiting for a response." Then, thinking out loud, "My guess is if we want to get to our clients within the next twenty-one days, we are going to have to go to court for an order requiring the government to let us visit sooner rather than later."

"We've got to do it, don't we?" I asked. "How long can a person survive on a hunger strike?" And then: "Wait a minute—how long have they been on this hunger strike in the first place?"

"I have no idea," Tom answered. "The only way to find out, short of speaking with the detainees themselves, is to ask the government, which is why Neil called. But, we need a plan."

Neil's phone call got nowhere. His request for permission to visit our clients at Guantánamo as soon as possible was denied with very little explanation. The DOJ's response was something along the lines of, "That's not convenient for us, because there's not enough room at the base." It was a long shot, but we asked if we could speak with our clients by phone with all the appropriate security measures in place. This was refused without any explanation. And so, for seemingly the millionth time, we went back to court. We went straight to the magistrate in charge of mediating disputes between detainees' counsel and the government lawyers. (There had been so many disputes regarding visits to Guantánamo, communications with clients and the like, that one magistrate had been assigned to oversee them all.) We asked Magistrate Kay to compel the government to let us visit Guantánamo during a time when we already knew that no other detainee counsel was scheduled to visit.

In the first court telephonic hearing, DOJ lawyers belittled the claims of a hunger strike, even though at the time, unbeknownst to us, five of our clients were on strike. Magistrate Kay called for another hearing the next day, ordering the government to come back with more information. According to the DOJ lawyers (after a bit of prodding from Magistrate Kay), three of our clients were on hunger strike; after more prodding by Magistrate Kay, the government agreed to let us go visit in ten days' time.

Ten days later, as we sat in the Fort Lauderdale airport, waiting for our Air Sunshine flight to be called, we learned from the government that two of our clients were in the hospital, one of whom had not even been previously named as being on hunger strike! We later learned that he had been on hunger strike since the beginning of August, along with Fawzi, who had also been on hunger strike since early August. The government informed us that we would not be allowed to see them at all. *What?* This was completely outrageous. The district court had ruled less than a year ago that the detainees had a right to counsel, which included reasonable access to their lawyers. We were their lawyers, and we were being prevented from seeing them without any reason given. From the worn-out plastic chairs in Terminal Four of the Fort Lauderdale airport, we called the magistrate, who held another telephonic hearing, ordering the government to go back and find a way to allow at least one counsel to visit the detainees in the hospital.

We arrived at Gitmo to find that the DOJ had indeed gotten it wrong: Five, not three, of our clients were on hunger strike, and all of them had been at it for much longer than the time frame given to us. *Did the DOJ lawyers just make a mistake?* I wondered. *Or were they intentionally falsifying this information? Or were they just passing on intentionally falsified information from Guantánamo authorities?* It was probably the latter. When you are only in contact with your clients once every several weeks, and they launch a hunger strike, it's alarming when the only information you can get about them is from an authority you can't trust.

Over the next two days we had three more hearings with the court via phone, talking with government lawyers who were incapable of providing details on the hospitalized Kuwaitis. Finally, Magistrate Kay ordered the government to produce somebody who *did* know the facts. That individual, insisting on anonymity during the telephonic hearing and referred to as "Dr. X" in the transcript we received, provided what we would soon discover were incorrect facts.

After no fewer than five telephonic hearings before the court, we were finally able to see all of our clients. The five men on hunger strike gave different reasons for joining the strike, but their feelings were the same: They had lost faith in the justice system and the ability of their lawyers to help them. They were mistreated by the guards, their religion had been abused, they wanted to be charged and given a chance to defend themselves, and they would rather be dead than be treated as less than animals. They wanted to be able to exercise some control over *something*, and refusing to eat was the only way to achieve that.

The strike was coordinated among more than just our five clients. The design of the prison at Guantánamo allowed several ways for detainees to communicate with one another. Sometimes they could hear each other through the vents, or they would yell loud enough through their mesh screens to their neighbors. Sometimes they were able to whisper hurriedly while passing each other coming to and from the detainee hospital, which meant that once again, like the details of the DVDs we'd been allowed to show our clients, word of a hunger strike spread quickly, and other detainees joined.

All of our hunger strikers looked pretty bad, but the two who had been in the hospital were being force-fed and looked close to death: Both had plastic tubes protruding from their noses for force-feeding; Al-Shammari, who was really tall and

didn't have much weight to lose in the first place, was frighten-
ingly skeletal—several guards had to assist him into the cell.
Fawzi looked pale and weak and bled from his nose intermit-
tently. Right away, Tom and I knew we had to at least *try* to
get them to eat again. We knew their families back in Kuwait
would be devastated to hear news of their declining health.

"Fawzi," I began, trying to smile at him. "How are you
feeling?"

"Oh, I feel very weak and nauseous all the time," he said. "I
am vomiting and having diarrhea." He didn't look at me as he
spoke, focusing on Tom.

"We see what you're trying to do here," Tom said. "But maybe
it would be a good idea to just try to eat one meal a day? Or at least
eat a little something every now and then? What will your father
say when we have to tell him what you are doing to yourself?"

Tom knew how strong the bond was between Fawzi and
Khalid, and he wasn't above mentioning it, especially if it
would get Fawzi to eat. I understood our clients' frustration; I
was frustrated, too, that I hadn't been able to do more for them.
But unlike them, I was able to return home to the U.S., to a
life that didn't revolve around occasional visits from a group
of attorneys.

"I just can't do it," Fawzi answered, almost apologetically.
"I refuse to eat because I have no other way of protesting my
treatment. If I eat, I condone the lie."

Then, the story came out. What had sparked the strike was
an event we'd heard about in bits and pieces from our clients

since we had first visited them at Guantánamo. One of the female interrogators, a woman named "Megan," had a habit of wearing tight, revealing clothing while asking questions of our (very devout Muslim) clients. They were often threatened with sexual abuse; in some instances, they were forced to strip naked in front of female guards. Other times, they'd been threatened with rape. Megan played a large role in these incidents. One client of ours reported that she was very sexually aggressive, and would blow smoke in his face, rub his neck, talk "dirty," and even go as far as to take off her shirt. Sometimes Megan would be joined by one or two other female interrogators, who would all use the same tactics—and when he would refuse their advances, they would belittle his manhood by claiming that they would "make him like women." If he became angry, Megan would laugh at him and leave him shackled to a chair for hours at a time.

Our clients were ashamed of the treatment they'd been receiving. It had been going on for sixteen months by the time the "Hunger to Death" strike, as the detainees called it, had begun. Our clients were simply too ashamed to tell us about the sexual abuse they'd received at the hands of the female guards—as well as being afraid of receiving worse treatment as retribution for speaking out—and only revealed what had been happening after we pressed them for details about why they'd decided to begin a hunger strike.

The abusive interrogations, this client said, had been increasing in frequency and strength, and one day he decided he'd had enough. The next time the guards came to his cell and told him that he had a "reservation" (Guantánamo-speak for an interrogation), he simply refused to go. I will never forget his explanation to me: "I would not let my own two feet take me to my abuse." In response, the Immediate Reaction Forces (IRF) team dragged him from his cell and beat him, forcing him to go to his interrogation. It didn't take long for news of his beating to spread throughout the prison camp, and that event— coupled with the beating of another detainee by the IRF—set off the widespread hunger strike.

By the time of our visit in mid-September, the government reported that there were one hundred and thirty people on hunger strike (defined as "when a detainee refuses nine meals over seventy-two hours"). By our counts, however, that number was significantly higher—between one hundred and seventy-five to one hundred and eighty-five—and the hunger strike for many detainees continued for almost five months. Those hunger-striking detainees who persisted in not eating ended up in the hospital, being force-fed.

The situation was grim. We responded immediately, conferring with our clients' families and going straight to court. We felt that the government had deliberately concealed information, and now it was refusing to keep us updated on the health of our clients. We asked the court to order the government to provide regular reports and medical records. We also asked that the two clients of ours who were being force-fed be allowed to speak with their families over the phone so that the families could counsel them to stop their strikes. We didn't feel this was an outrageous request, because we had learned that detainees at Gitmo who had been charged with war crimes had been allowed a phone call home, whereas our clients, who had never been charged with any crime and were losing weight despite the force-feeding, were being refused the same opportunity.

The court denied our requests.

I began researching hunger strikes by prisoners and contacted doctors who were experts, trying to understand the nature of hunger strikes—why people hunger strike, the problems involved with force-feeding, and ethical issues implicated. As I read more about hunger strikes, I began to feel very strange and uncomfortable about what we were doing or not doing. I had read several papers on the medical ethics involved, including one by the World Medical Association (WMA), and the position was that no patient, even a prisoner, should ever be force-fed. If a patient wants to die, it should be his or her decision. It's a matter of respecting the autonomy of his or her body.

I thought about Fawzi and the other hunger strikers who had said they would rather die than eat. What that meant for Fawzi was that if he got his way, if his feeding tube was removed and he continued his hunger strike, he would die. And by the looks of him, I didn't think it would take very long. It was pretty obvious to me that the only thing keeping him alive was that feeding tube. And he wanted to be rid of it. We were his lawyers; we were supposed to be working on his behalf, in his best interests. *Who were we to decide what his best interests were?* Shouldn't we be petitioning the court to stop the force-feeding?

"If Fawzi wants to die," I said back in D.C. behind the closed doors of Tom's office, "we should let him die." I was devastated, but firmly believed that it should be Fawzi's right to determine his fate, should he decide to see his hunger strike through to the end. It had only been a week since we'd been back from Guantánamo, and the shock of seeing five of our clients on hunger strike, two of them dangerously close to death or serious illness, had not left either of us.

Tom didn't want to see Fawzi die, either, and was just as determined to save him—at any cost. "That's not what the families want, Kristine." Tom had a close relationship with Fawzi and was particularly devastated to see him so weak, sick, and hopeless.

"I know, Tom. But who's our client here? Is it Fawzi, or his family? What about what Fawzi wants?"

"What are we going to do—ask the court to let him die?" Tom shouted. He was angry, not at me, but at the situation, the court, the DOJ lawyers, the government, and everything in between.

"Who are you to decide what's best for Fawzi? Who made you God?" I was yelling, and suddenly, I was crying, too. Tom jumped up to hug me. We were both upset. Tom and I both knew that we had an ethical obligation to do as our client wished. And yet, we couldn't bring ourselves to be the ones to seal Fawzi's fate—a slow death in a cell at the Guantánamo Bay detention center. Had we known we'd be having a conversation of this magnitude when we first met with the Kuwaitis, in which someone's life was in our hands, maybe we wouldn't have agreed to take their case. But there we were, neck deep in a case that had seemed impossible at every turn, where every decision we made seemed to have either substantial consequences or no impact at all on somebody else's welfare. It was getting to us.

We began preparing to take another trip to Guantánamo as soon as we could, asking the government if we could bring DVDs made by the families, advising their sons to stop their hunger strike. Although we'd been allowed to bring DVDs with us on earlier visits to Gitmo, this time, the government turned us down. Our visit in October was even more difficult than the last. Fawzi and Al-Shammari were even worse off than before. Fawzi, though being force-fed, was still losing weight and was down to about a hundred and ten pounds. His weight would drop to ninety-seven pounds within two weeks.

"The feeding tube is just another instrument of torture," Fawzi told us. "They use restraints on me, force my head back, and shove in tubes that are too big; they make me bleed and vomit. I just want to have some control over my own body. It's all I have left."

We listened to everything Fawzi had to say, took detailed notes, and drafted an affidavit with him, which he signed for us to submit to the court. Fawzi himself was conflicted; he wanted better conditions and a chance to prove his innocence, and, at the same time, he wanted us to petition the court to have the feeding tubes removed so he could die. We left Guantánamo after that trip, not knowing if we would ever see Fawzi again. Our return to D.C. was grim.

In the meantime, I continued my quest to get as much information as possible, consulting with several doctors. One doctor in particular had just the kind of background we knew would be persuasive to a judge. Dr. Stephen Xenakis was a psychiatrist and retired brigadier general, the exact combination of medical expertise and military knowledge that we needed. I felt sufficiently at ease with him to confide my ethical dilemma: respecting Fawzi's autonomy and his right to die, while at the same time recognizing that his parents didn't want him to die, we didn't want him to die, and that Fawzi himself probably didn't want to die either. But again, maybe he did; how were we supposed to know?

Dr. Xenakis pointed out the WMA's Malta Declaration, which states that doctors are obligated to try to determine the patient's true desires; if a patient is making a competent or informed decision to hunger strike, medical personnel are obligated to follow the patient's decision. They cannot ethically force that patient to accept nutrition. Generally, according to Dr. Xenakis, in the case of a hunger strike, the patient gets to speak to a religious guide from his chosen faith; his family helps talk him through his decision; often, a second opinion is called for; and then a medical board of ethics is convened to address the life-or-death consequences of a hunger-strike situation. It is a long process of decision making and consultation. Unfortunately for Fawzi (and for us), what "normally" happens in the case of a hunger strike was not happening in our case, as Fawzi wasn't allowed any of those things—access to religious guidance or to his family, or a doctor he trusted. Basically, we decided, Fawzi wasn't given the opportunity to make an informed decision.

We began compiling affidavits by doctors, had the affidavits our clients had written at Guantánamo cleared by the privilege team, and began drafting our brief—our last shot at trying to help our clients have some say in how their hunger strikes progressed. All we were asking for was that we be provided medical updates and records so that we could be informed, plus one lousy phone call between the detainees and their families, so that family members could try to persuade them to stop their strike. In our motion to the court, Fawzi had asked us to include in the motion a request that he not be force-fed, and that he be allowed to pursue his hunger strike if he so chose.

We were pretty sure the courts wouldn't order the removal of his feeding tube, and we told Fawzi so, but he insisted. We added that to the motion with much hesitation, along with a caveat: that we be allowed to consult with Fawzi's father, Khalid, who was also a plaintiff in the case. We had one more visit to Guantánamo, at which point only Fawzi was on hunger strike, as Al-Shammari had been released, maintaining his hunger strike until he reached a hospital in Kuwait. We also had one more hearing before the court with testimony from yet another doctor from the Guantánamo hospital, whose name was classified. He reported that Fawzi was in good health: "Fawzi has lost weight but we think that was due to stress and not the effects of the nasogastric feeding. He gained some weight back and I saw him yesterday, smiling and interactive. Fawzi is fine," he said. "I just saw him doing twenty pull-ups."

"That's funny," Neil said, "because the last time we saw Fawzi, he was using a walker just to get around."

We were incredulous. It was yet another shock in a series of shocking misrepresentations. We had requested a hearing because Fawzi's weight and potassium levels were so low that he could have suffered cardiac arrest if he was not closely monitored. At five-foot-nine and ninety-eight pounds (according to the medical records Fawzi had been able to procure from a sympathetic soul at the detainee hospital), Fawzi was far from healthy to us. But the court disagreed, stating that the team at Guantánamo was doing "everything they could do," and it wasn't their fault that Fawzi was losing weight. For me, that was probably the most depressing moment of the entire time we'd spent working on the detainees' case, the culmination of all of the requests we'd been making, and it was by far the most significant. This guy's life was at stake, and the courts were basically patting the entire military team at Guantánamo on the back and saying, "Great job!"

By our next visit, Fawzi *had* managed to gain a little bit of weight, and was around one hundred and two pounds. Seeing what he was putting himself through, the treatment he had received, it was hard to have faith that the government was doing *anything* right—regardless of what the U.S. courts might think. Fawzi reported that the government had flown in several six-point restraint chairs to use on the twenty detainees who had continued their hunger strikes and were now being held in the hospital at all times. Within a week, he said, the number of detainees on hunger strike dropped from twenty to four.

"They put me in the chair," he said. "I could hear screams in the next room. It sounded like that prisoner was in *serious* pain."

Tom and I exchanged glances. *How awful could a scream possibly sound to seem worse than what Fawzi has already lived through?* I wondered, immediately deciding not to ask, because I most definitely didn't want to know the answer.

Realizing we were waiting for him to continue, Fawzi said, "That's when I decided to give up my hunger strike. I did not do this to be tortured."

Looking at Fawzi, and seeing how weak he still was, even after finally ending his hunger strike, I wondered what the government could possibly need six-point restraining chairs for; certainly it wouldn't take more than one fairly strong person to hold Fawzi down in his weakened state. He was on the brink of death, for heaven's sake! That was the reason given for force-feeding him and other detainees to begin with.

I didn't know it then, but that was one of the last times I would see Fawzi. He is still, today, being held at the detention center at Guantánamo Bay without charges or trial. The work I did with Shearman & Sterling for the detainees at Gitmo is work that I am very proud of—and yet, it was painful for me, a proud patriot, to have lost faith in my government. I feel very strongly about being proud to be an American, and in my eyes, simply the way our prisoners had been treated—like animals instead of human beings—was enough to make me feel that we'd lost our standing in the world. We had been a leader and a champion of human rights and the rule of law, but at Guantánamo those laws had been discarded; as a guard told one of our clients, "Here, the law is thrown into the sea."

The hunger strikes at Guantánamo ended an era for me and for Shearman; after Fawzi decided to end his hunger strike, we were essentially in a holding pattern due in no small part to legislation that had been passed in December 2005. During the fall of 2005, Congress began debating legislation offered by the conservatives that would have the effect of reversing the *Rasul* decision; that is, stripping the Guantánamo detainees of their right to challenge their detention through habeas petitions. Senator Lindsey Graham made statements on the Senate floor essentially saying that the "enemy" should not be getting DVDs, among other things, and we knew it was going to be a huge battle to preserve the earlier decision of the Supreme Court.

Moderates, as much as they didn't like the Detainee Treatment Act (DTA), had their constituents to think about, and their constituents didn't want "terrorists" getting DVDs or challenging their detentions in court. Along with other lawyers representing Guantánamo detainees—people from NGOs like Human Rights Watch, The Constitution Project, law professors and deans, even retired military officers and former judges—I wrote letters and spent a lot of time on the Hill, meeting with staffers and representatives, educating them on the legal issues involved in the DTA, explaining the far-reaching effects such a law would have.

I had met Marty Meehan, representative from the state of Massachusetts, and Jim Moran, congressman from the Commonwealth of Virginia, and spoken with them on a few panels about torture. They introduced me to other representatives: John Conyers from Michigan, Tom Davis from Virginia, and Ike Skelton from Missouri. Once again, I was learning that lawyering involved so much more than brief-writing and depositions. Unfortunately, the DTA passed on December 30, 2005, putting a halt to our Guantánamo cases, and allowing the D.C. Circuit Court to request more briefing on the legal issues. Our litigation was on hold.

By mid-January 2006, our motions for better conditions were just sitting in the district court (the lowest court), and we were waiting for the D.C. Circuit (the middle appellate court) to make a decision—any decision—on the appeal of the larger legal issue of whether or not the detainees could challenge their detentions. We were satisfied that our clients' lives were no longer in such imminently grave danger as they had been during the hunger strikes (even though we certainly felt they were in at least some danger for the duration of their stays at

Guantánamo), but now we had time to focus on other things. Or, at least, I did.

Frankly, I was tired. I had "Guantánamo fatigue." I had spent a busy summer flying back and forth to Guantánamo, filing motions and briefs, speaking to the press, and speaking at conferences. For me, it was Guantánamo night and day, day in and day out. Somehow that summer, however, I also managed to train for something that was becoming a great passion of mine: a triathlon.

I had switched from marathons to triathlons; it was my second year of competing in them, and I loved it. I trained hard with a running group at six a.m., did "bricks" (a bike and run) with my triathlon friends, Karen and Lynn, swam as little as possible, cycled with Bryan (who still liked me despite all my anti-Bush activity) on the weekends, and ran every night I spent at Guantánamo, usually joined by Tom, Jared, and Neil, who called them our "forced runs." For the first time, I placed in my age group in a triathlon, an accomplishment I would go on to achieve several more times in future races. Bryan would accompany me to many of my triathlons, cheering me on throughout the race and bellowing out at the finish line, "Move it, Huskey!" Spending so much personal time doing something that motivated me filled me with a bit of pride; and yes, it was competitive. It made me stop and think about my job at Shearman—it really was my life, and Guantánamo and the detainees had become my life, too. I decided, that summer, to start investigating career options outside the firm.

For an attorney, once you reach a certain level of seniority within a big law firm, you have to make a decision. You're either up or you're out. In a nutshell, you have to decide: Do you want to go for partner (that means an all-out, 150 percent commitment to doing whatever it takes to make partner), or do you want to change jobs? For me, it wasn't an easy choice. I had learned so much during my time at Shearman. I'd traveled a lot, worked with amazing people, and been given some amazing opportunities. I really liked my work, but the lifestyle at a big firm like Shearman meant that, although I had been right about the difference between Shearman's work environment and other law firms in a place like NYC, I still had little spare time to pursue the other hobbies I found so fulfilling, like running marathons and competing in triathlons (and dating Bryan—although by then he was much more than a hobby). Eventually, I decided to go part-time at Shearman (which really meant that I'd be billing about forty hours a week instead of eighty or more), and take a chance at getting into the academic side of law. I wanted to teach.

I had done a brief stint as a visiting professor at a law school in New Zealand when Shearman allowed me to take a month-long sabbatical, and I'd really enjoyed it. I managed to get two adjunct teaching gigs—one at Howard University Law School, and one at George Washington University Law School. It was a really busy time in my life from a work standpoint, as I had three different, fairly demanding jobs, but in order to make the transition from attorney in a law firm to academia, I needed to gain experience in the classroom. My ultimate goal—finding a full-time teaching job at a law school—started to come into focus.

I'd discovered that I had an aptitude for teaching, and also that, surprisingly, I really enjoyed it. I found law students so refreshing, so enamored with and hopeful about the law. It was quite a change from working at a big law firm where lawyers can become somewhat jaded after a series of failed motions and getting nowhere. And not only was I beginning to realize I had possibly chosen a new law path for myself that would be really rewarding, but life in general was becoming more important to me once again. I had been dating Bryan now for almost three years. I was falling in love with him; for the first time since my divorce, I felt I'd found someone I could truly spend the rest of my life with. (Of course, it would take another three years for that day to come, but who's counting?) For so long, my life had been consumed by my work; it had been Tom and Neil and the twelve Kuwaitis at Guantánamo. For the first time in a really long while, I was starting to think about myself and what I wanted the next part of my life to be about.

I knew I couldn't give up the human rights work I'd become so passionate about, so when I got a call in March 2006 from Rick Wilson, the director of the International Human Rights Law Clinic at American University (AU), Washington College of Law (WCL), I was understandably thrilled. I'd met Rick a while back; he and his clinic at AU had been representing a detainee at Guantánamo, the notorious Omar Khadr (more about him later). All of the lawyers in the country who had clients at Gitmo eventually became friendly, or at least knew each other in some way or another.

"Hi, Kristine," Rick began. "We've met a few times at some of the habeas counsel meetings, and we also met at the Inter-American Commission for Human Rights hearing over the Guantánamo detainees. Do you remember?"

Remember? Of course I remembered him. Professor Rick Wilson was an icon in the field of human rights and legal clinical education. I had heard of him and his clinic since I began speaking on human rights a few years earlier. I couldn't believe he was calling *me.*

"Sure, yes, of course I remember you," I replied, trying to sound calm.

"I'm calling because I heard through the grapevine that you've been teaching as an adjunct in GW's Human Rights Clinic with Arturo Carrillo. I know Arturo—good guy. I was wondering if you'd be interested in applying for a fellowship-type position with AU's Human Rights Clinic. Our current practitioner-in-residence, Janie, will be leaving, so the position will be open beginning this summer. I thought of you right away."

I didn't hesitate. "Rick! Of *course* I'd be interested," I said, thinking to myself in amazement that sometimes things just seem to fall into place. "First, let me tell you how thrilled I am to even be asked to apply. This really is quite an honor. Just tell me what the application process is like, and I'll get started right away." I must have said "thrilled" and "honored" at least three times each. I later e-mailed him to thank him for his personal call. Of course, I did have to apply first before I got the job.

The practitioner-in-residence position at AU was essentially a fellowship rather than a tenure-track position. It was an interim teaching position on a year-to-year contract basis that allowed a newbie law professor to gain academic experience and work on scholarship (i.e., publish something) in preparation for entering the teaching market. And, believe it or not, getting a law professor job isn't easy. In fact, it's just as competitive as getting an associate position at a top law firm, except that there are fewer positions available and relatively no turnover. How many old white guys still teach at the nations' top law schools? Plenty. Getting a fellowship at a prestigious school like American University would be a great foundation on which to begin building my teaching career, but in no way would it guarantee me a job at a top law school, or even at an obscure law school in the middle of nowhere.

I applied for the job, still not completely certain if a professorship was what I was looking for, but willing to give it a chance. I certainly was not making any assumptions that I'd be given an offer. I met Rick and his colleague, Muneer Ahmad, in person, and then went through a series of interviews with the dean, via telephone. (I was in Vienna at the time with my students from Howard, who were competing in a World Trade Organization moot court competition. You just can't get the travel bug out of me no matter what job I have!)

When I got back to D.C., I was offered the job. I had a few sleepless nights before accepting the position, and then the plan was set: I would be leaving Shearman by the beginning of May. Tom and I planned one last visit to Guantánamo for me, in which we broke the news to our clients that I would be leaving the firm in order to teach. It was bittersweet for me and for the clients; for the most part, they were happy for me. They knew how hard I had worked for them, but they were still sad that I wouldn't be coming back to visit them. And, to be honest, so was I. I knew that the families of our Kuwaitis were on the brink of deciding that they no longer wanted Shearman to represent their sons. It was not an uncommon result after years of litigation that had produced few results. We had broken a lot of ground with our work at Guantánamo, but the families were hoping that a new firm with a fresh outlook might generate more results. (Of course, Tom always liked to point out that we did, in fact, produce the result of a win at the Supreme Court, which was certainly nothing to sneeze at.)

So, for me, having to lose contact with my clients at Guantánamo, which would have happened either way, wasn't a huge factor in my decision to leave for American University. I was more concerned about the 70 percent pay cut and whether I would be as fulfilled by a job that required much more teaching and much less litigation. Luckily, I'd prepared for the eventuality of not going for partner at Shearman by saving up a little nest egg. This made it even more feasible for me to leave my high-paying corporate law gig for a teaching position.

What really intrigued me about joining the clinic at AU was that I'd still be working on Guantánamo litigation. Rick and his clinic were representing a Gitmo detainee who was becoming an increasingly controversial figure—and they needed help. Originally just one of many enemy combatants at Gitmo, Omar Khadr was eventually charged with war crimes, but that wasn't what made him famous. His notoriety came from the fact that he'd been picked up at age fifteen and brought to the detention center when he was just sixteen years old. He had received no special juvenile treatment, either in the manner in which he was detained or in the way in which he was ultimately charged. By the time I started at AU, Omar was twenty-one years old, and had spent a quarter of his life in a cell at Guantánamo Bay.

Here I am, headed back to Gitmo to meet another client—except this time, it's different, I thought. *This time, I actually have a client who's been accused of war crimes.*

12

This Is a Man's World

NOT SURPRISINGLY, I DECIDED TO CELEBRATE MY DEPARTURE from the corporate law world and my entrance to academia with a trip to a faraway land. I was on top of the world after having landed such a sought-after teaching fellowship with the human rights clinic at American University; plus, I had managed to last eight long years at a big law firm (imagine the number of billable hours I'd racked up!). I deserved a reward.

I decided to go all out. I booked a trekking trip in the Andes Mountains in Peru, specifically, the Cordillera Huay-huash Range, as in the movie *Touching the Void*, where the mountain climber nearly dies. Yes, I know. I am always up for a challenge. It was the antithesis of the backpacking trip Doug and I had taken all those years ago. This time, instead of consulting the *Lonely Planet* guide and drifting along from place to place for months on end, I paid a travel company to take care of the logistics for me, and spent three weeks hiking and camping with other trekkers. (Unfortunately, Bryan couldn't take off four weeks from work, and I wasn't willing to cut my hard-earned trip short.). And, it was cushy camping—we had donkeys to carry our food; a camp crew member would come by every morning offering coffee or tea; and when we reached our destination at the end of each day, the crew would set up our tents for us, prepare and serve dinner, and clean up the dishes (what luxury!).

The camping may have been "easy," but the hiking was difficult. We trekked for about nine hours a day, and crossed three passes that were over 14,000 feet, one that was 15,000, and another that was 16,000! Three weeks in the great outdoors was just what I needed to clear my mind and focus on the next phase of my life—although, I must admit, my body wasn't quite as cooperative about sleeping on the ground as it had been when I was younger! I think I must have gone soft after all of those Shearman trips staying at places like the Four Seasons and the Waldorf-Astoria. I spent twenty-one days sleeping on a pad in a sleeping bag in frigid temperatures, with no shower, and a porta-potty for a toilet. I was ready to be back in a hotel with a fluffy bed by the end of the trek.

The trip began uneventfully. The Huayhuash Range is magnificent, and much less trekked than the other ranges due to its harsh terrain and multitude of soaring peaks. I was thrilled to be in Peru.

The drama didn't start until the third week of the trip. Our group—there were about eight of us—were following behind our guides, in a line. We were at about 13,000 feet, where small villages or lone huts dot the landscape; the mountain people who live in them are descendants of the Incas. As we climbed out of a valley, a runaway cow came charging down the path at us (where it came from, I have no idea). Luckily, we all managed to jump out of the way. Or so I thought. I'd assumed the cow had kept running, but everything was so chaotic I didn't even hear the cow as it turned around and came barreling back up the path—directly at me. It charged me, and when it made contact, I became a gymnast. I did a full back flip over the cow's back, landing on the ground behind it, flat on my back. My neck snapped back, and my head hit the ground, which was covered in rocks and small boulders. Of course, I had no idea that I'd flown so gracefully through the air (and landed not-so-gracefully); it all happened so fast that I really had no time to react until I was suddenly on my back, face to the sky.

Later, the head guide told me that he had watched the whole thing. "My stomach sank, Kristine," he said. "I thought, 'Oh my God, we are going to need a helicopter to evacuate you out.'"

I had landed with such force and flown through the air at such a strange angle that our entire group of trekkers thought I'd broken my neck, or my back—at least until I sat up, dazed, and immediately started crying. I was in shock, what can I say? Fortunately, my daypack, which was filled with an extra fleece, rain jacket, and gloves in case the temperature dropped, had softened my landing, probably saving me from cracking a rib, or worse.

My body reacted immediately, too: Right away my shin started to swell, and I had huge contusions on my arms from my hard landing. "That's the last time I wear a red shirt on this trip," I joked. The guides took great care of me; once they'd determined that I was not seriously injured (although we all knew I was going to be ridiculously sore in a few hours), the guides ran down to the river and soaked some towels for my shin, to help bring down the swelling. I still have scar tissue on my shin from that bruise.

Meanwhile, the cow was pretty pleased with herself. She was sitting about twenty-five feet away—on top of my sunglasses, I might add—chewing her cud. It could've been a hallucination, but I swear she was smirking. Luckily for me, I was basically fine. For the rest of the day, I rode on the ambulance horse (the horse our guides had brought along just in case one of us managed to get injured in a place that couldn't be accessed by an emergency helicopter). There was no way I was going to let some crazy cow keep me from completing my hard-earned trek! Two days later, we reached the point in our trek where those of us who were willing and hearty could join the guides in summiting a nearby mountain peak. Of course I was in! And I was the only "tourist trekker" willing to go. I wrapped up my leg in an ace bandage and set off with two of our guides at four in the morning, with ropes and crampons and the other supplies a person needs to summit a 17,000-foot mountain peak.

On the way, I wasn't sure I was going to make it. At some points, the slope was covered in icy snow, and even with my crampons strapped to my feet for traction, it was all I could do to keep going. The air was so thin and the path very steep. I was thankful the three of us were tied together by a rope, with me in the middle. When I looked up, all I could see was a wall of white and the back of Jorge (our Peruvian guide who could climb like a mountain goat); behind me was Rob, the American guide who worked for the travel company I had booked with.

"Okay (*huff*) . . . Do you think Jorge (*puff*) can just give us some more (*wheeze*) rest time?" I asked Rob when he caught up to me. The higher we climbed, the more we had to stop and rest. We were "resting" just then, but Jorge was still out in front of us, making us look bad. Rob was breathing hard (not as hard as me, but hard nonetheless). *Oh thank God*, I thought. *Maybe he needs a longer rest, too!*

"You're doing great, Kristine! How are you feeling?" Rob was a superb guide—encouraging and friendly, and he knew a ton about the surrounding flora and fauna.

"Well (*huff*), umm (*puff*), I feel like my quads are on fire. Can I get a hit of your chocolate bar? I need some sugar. I need something. I'm flagging over here. I'm dying," I said as fast as I could, given my panting. Rob looked at me with a smile.

"Okay, I'm joking," I said. "I'm fine. But can I still have some of your chocolate?"

We succeeded in reaching the top of El Diablo Mudo; at just over 17,000 feet, it definitely felt like the devil's work.

When I got back to civilization a few days later, to the hotel in Huaraz where we had begun the trip at a measly 10,000 feet, I finally got a chance to look in the mirror and survey my injuries from the impromptu cow fight. My entire back side—shoulders to thighs—was painted with lovely shades of purples and blues. But I was lucky; I would heal. After the trek, I went alone to the famed ancient city of Machu Picchu, which was truly amazing. Though I had missed Bryan, the trip turned out to be another great adventure that had made me stronger for all its challenges.

When I returned, I didn't have much time to adjust to my new life in academia. I had left Shearman in May, spent a month in Peru, and started at AU in July. Law professors that teach and work in a law clinic pretty much work year-round. It's like a law firm that teaches students how to be lawyers, with real clients. A clinic represents people who can't otherwise afford legal counsel, with the students basically making the counseling decisions, planning legal strategy, and writing the briefs, all under the guidance and mentorship of the professors. The clinic model appealed to me because I'd still get to practice litigation, which I enjoyed, but I'd get to do it while working with law students, teaching and mentoring them, which I also enjoyed. I was thrilled to be embarking on a new career, and I knew I'd been lucky to be offered such a great opportunity.

Half of the cases we handled at AU were immigration cases, usually asylum cases, like the case two of my energetic and ambitious students handled on behalf of a woman from the Democratic Republic of Congo. She had been raped and beaten by soldiers for her political activism and could hardly talk about her experiences when my students first met her. But with their gentle persuasion and patient efforts, she was able to testify on the stand, winning asylum at the end of the hearing, which my students handled all by themselves (with me always at elbow's reach).

The other half of the cases we handled in the clinic were international human rights cases. Two of my students helped draft the complaint that was eventually brought against Yahoo! for its complicity in human rights abuses in China. Another team submitted a report to a United Nations committee on behalf of a persecuted ethnic group in Ethiopia. But one of the main reasons I'd been hired was because the human rights clinic at WCL was representing a detainee at Gitmo: Omar Khadr, the child soldier from Canada. One of my first tasks as a new member of the clinic faculty, a couple months into my first semester, was a familiar assignment: I went back to Guantánamo, with Rick.

Visiting Gitmo while representing a detainee who's actually been charged with war crimes was a completely different experience from my previous visits. To begin with, it felt a lot like my very first visit: There was a lot of nervous anticipation, a lot of wondering about how we would be received by Omar. He was twenty-one by then, but he'd been at Gitmo since he was sixteen; he'd gone from being a teenager to trying to be a man, and he'd been a difficult client, understandably. Rick and Muneer Ahmad, the other professor in the clinic (a strategic litigator and brilliant scholar), tried to explain the situation to me. The last trip they'd made to see Omar had been pretty rocky, and Muneer wasn't sure whether they'd really been fired or if Omar had just been upset. Rick and Muneer were hoping that a fresh face would be a nice change for him—that maybe he would be responsive to a new lawyer on the team.

It was a huge shock to me, how different our treatment was when we arrived at Guantánamo. Omar had been one of the few detainees to actually have charges for war crimes brought against him, and somehow that seemed to gain his legal counsel a lot of extra clout. For starters, we could rent a car—something that the Shearman team had never been allowed to do. We also got to stay on the other side of the base—Windward Side, where the military stayed—so we didn't have to take the ferry across every morning, and we weren't required to have a military escort accompany us everywhere we went. I was amazed to find that it wasn't just the legal counsel who was treated differently; Omar's experience at Gitmo was also somewhat different from what I'd been used to hearing from my Kuwaiti clients: Sometimes he was allowed magazines and books. It made me a little sad for my former clients, who had been detained at Guantánamo for several years before the government began to provide them with reading materials other than the Koran—and even then, they were heavily censored and very selective.

On our first day, Omar refused to meet with us. In response, Rick wrote him a letter explaining that he'd brought a new lawyer with him—a lawyer that had worked with the Kuwaitis. The notoriety that came with being counsel for the Kuwaitis must've intrigued Omar, because on the second day, he agreed to see us. It was another strange experience for me. Instead of going to Camp Echo for our meeting, we went to Camp Five, where Omar's permanent cell was located. But we didn't meet in his cell; we met in a "visitor's cell," some kind of holding cell.

Before we were even allowed into the prison, we had to go through a metal detector and let a guard rifle through our papers, looking for any documents that weren't "related to our legal representation." Since the guard clearly wasn't a lawyer, I was kind of wondering how he could possibly know what he was looking for (of course, I didn't ask).

This reminded me of one of my last visits to our Kuwaiti clients. Tom had given me a pocket-sized Constitution which I carried around—still do—in my purse. When the guard searched my purse at the entrance of Camp Echo, looking for physical contraband (like a nail file) or documents that were not related to my case (per the protective order, we were allowed to bring in only documents related to the legal case), he pulled out my Constitution. The air thickened with tension, and I wondered if he would try to confiscate it. I could practically see the sweat forming on his brow; his mind was working furiously. He knew what it was—it said "The Constitution" on the cover in red, white, and blue, after all, but it had been in my purse, not in the file with my other legal documents. The question was whether or not he would take *my* Constitution and tell me I couldn't bring it in to my clients. The symbolism was so obvious, I could have screamed. After a few agonizing minutes, the soldier put it back in my purse and handed it over to me.

Omar was waiting for us in a relatively small room, about three by six feet. Probably the most remarkable thing, to me, was that he wasn't shackled. He wasn't handcuffed. He'd been charged with crimes of war—murder, conspiracy, and terrorism—and yet he was granted more freedoms and less physical restraints than his fellow detainees, who were only a short walk away and hadn't been charged *with anything*. It didn't make any sense to me, but I kept my observations to myself. It was Guantánamo, upside down all over again.

What I will always remember about Omar is how grown-up he seemed, despite his youth. It was depressing that at the age of twenty-one, he'd spent a quarter of his life—years that should've been some of his best—in a supermax military prison facility at Guantánamo Bay, with men ten to twenty years older than him. He'd never had a girlfriend. He hadn't seen or even been allowed to talk to his mom or any member of his family in five years. Even *convicted* rapists and serial killers in civilian prisons get some kind of familial contact. Omar got nothing, and he hadn't even seen the inside of a courtroom. It was heartbreaking. By the time I met him, Omar had pretty much resigned himself to the fact that Guantánamo was his life. He thought he'd be there forever, and he was good at putting on a brave face.

"Omar," I began, in my most understanding tone, "we can help you through this. We can help you challenge these charges, these proceedings, in a way that allows you to protest that the military commissions are wrong. We agree with you that they are unfair. They are terrible." Even the new Military Commissions Act of 2006, just passed by Congress, is inadequate and unfair. This legislation dictated new procedures for military trials for war crimes, under which Omar would face trial. We spent the first thirty minutes of the visit explaining the new legislation to him, pointing out the problems that he might encounter.

"I know, I know—I understand," said Omar. "I'm sure you can do a good job." He sounded more like an adult than a young man just out of his teens. Despite his words of confidence, Omar didn't want to have anything to do with the military trials at all, even if he would be forced to face one. I didn't blame him. The trial procedures were grossly unfair; I wouldn't have wanted to have anything to do with one, either. In some ways, I admired him for taking a position he felt was one of principle, even if it did seem foolish and unrealistic.

"They're going to make you participate, whether you want to or not," I said, trying to be as gentle as possible while still remaining firm. "If you work with us, you can tell your story in the way that you want, with some control."

It was the wrong thing to say—I had only triggered his teenage bravado. "I'm fine here," he said, giving me a half-hearted smile. Then, gesturing to the cell, Omar said, "I like it here. Guantánamo is fine."

Realizing I'd steered our conversation in a bad direction, I made an attempt at humor. "I feel like I'm being broken up with on my first date," I said.

Omar did not officially fire us, but it was clear he couldn't have cared less whether we came to visit him or not. We continued to work with Omar's assigned military lawyers (JAGs) back in the States, who told us that Omar had conveyed to them in a later visit that he didn't mind if we assisted them. I realized that, more than ever, lawyers didn't have much of an ability to impact their clients' lives while they were being held at Gitmo. It was just the latest in a long line of frustrating realizations I'd had since I started working with the Kuwaitis in 2002. It's hard to avoid self-doubt when you feel so helpless.

I was also starting to realize how much men dominated the field I had chosen: Most of the JAG lawyers representing detainees were men; the majority of professors doing Guantánamo-related work were men; and every time I spoke on a panel at a conference where the subject was the military commissions, the laws of war, or Guantánamo in general, I was surrounded by male lawyers, male military officers, male government policy wonks, and male academics. And, of course, during my visits to Guantánamo, I rarely came into contact with any females.

After such a disappointing visit to Guantánamo, though, things were looking up. I was still working on the Guantánamo litigation, but I was also, finally, getting things going in the classroom. While I'd realized a while before that one of my favorite tasks at Shearman was working with the newest associates as a mentor, I had no idea how quickly I'd take to teaching. Teaching is often about performing and I guess I'd done a lot of that my whole life. Learning how to be a professor and how to teach was hard—don't get me wrong. But my students were so enthusiastic, so intrigued by the law, that it was hard to keep at least a little bit of that excitement from rubbing off on me. And my colleagues in the human rights clinic—Rick, Muneer, and Jayesh, a "fellow" just like me—provided an atmosphere that was nurturing, welcoming, and laid-back. Academia encouraged deep intellectual exploration and long, almost too long, discussions about the law and what it meant. It was such a change from the daily grind and quick pace at Shearman, and it felt really good to know that I had made the right choice in leaving law-firm life for a chance to teach.

Personally, however, my life was anything but constant. My new teaching schedule had given me the freedom I sought in order to have a regular training schedule to do triathlons. I had decided that my priorities needed a bit of a change: Instead of fitting my training time in around my grueling agenda as a litigator, I now got to plan my teaching schedule around my training! I almost never made it to the office before ten a.m., and I didn't feel a damn bit guilty about it. It was amazingly freeing and intensely satisfying; for the first time since I'd lived in Angola, I had true weekends off. Even when I'd been at Columbia, I had spent most of my weekend nights bartending. I was finally becoming the well-rounded lawyer I wanted to be—a lawyer who could pursue other things besides the decision she wanted in a courtroom.

In contrast, my relationship with Bryan was full of both sunshine and rain. Oh, it was a good relationship, as far as he knew, but I was becoming increasingly frustrated. Along with my newfound freedoms (weekends!), I'd come to realize that what I really wanted was something I had been putting off for a long time so that I could focus on my career: I wanted a family. And, truthfully, I wanted it with Bryan. I finally had the time to take stock of my life, to reorganize my priorities, and I discovered, somewhat to my surprise (I could hardly believe that I had let so much of my life pass by without giving this topic more serious thought), that the one thing I really wanted out of life was to become a mother. Here I was at thirty-nine, just waking up to the fact that I wanted a baby! And I couldn't imagine wanting to start a family with anyone other than the man who had managed to capture my heart after the heartbreak I'd suffered from my first marriage.

Although I wanted to marry Bryan and start a family together, the timing wasn't great for him. He wasn't ready for marriage, he wasn't ready to have a family, and he certainly wasn't ready to commit without being 100 percent certain. It was an argument we began to have more and more frequently. Once I realized that I wanted more from life than just a (great) career, it became all I could think about when I was with him. Where our relationship had once been a steady one, in which we were both extremely busy professionals who put our careers first but still managed to really enjoy each other's company, it started to become a relationship in which he wanted to preserve the status quo, and I wanted to take things to the next level. The dynamic was asymmetrical. I wanted a solid commitment. I wanted to talk about trying to have a baby. I wanted it all, and I felt like my window of opportunity was quickly closing—it was either get serious now, or let me go so that I could try to find the kind of relationship that would give me what I was looking for.

Needless to say, that was a painful time for me. I knew Bryan loved me, and I could understand his hesitation to a point, but we'd been together for more than four years, and I felt like he ought to know by this point whether or not he wanted to make a commitment to me. I hadn't changed; I was still the same person I'd been for the course of our relationship, but my outlook had changed, and I began to sink into a deep depression. It wasn't made any easier by the fact that most of my closest friends were all married, including my sister, and some were starting families of their own.

I was meeting "the girls" for our monthly dinner at a new restaurant, an event I always looked forward to, but this time I was dreading it. Karen, Julie, Jenny Lee, and I had all worked at Shearman, and we'd all, over time, managed to leave for greener pastures, but we still got together once a month. They were my girl fix—filling me in on celebrity gossip (most of the time I had no idea who they were talking about), sharing fashion ideas, discussing sex (okay, maybe I was the one who always brought up that topic). They were all incredibly smart lawyers, *and* they were fashionistas, flirts, and funny at the same time. They had all managed to get married, Julie and Jenny Lee were pregnant, and Karen was probably going to break the news any day. It would have been harder to be around them if not for their constant support of me and my goals, both career-related and personal.

"So, Bryan and I are supposed to go to this wedding in Florida soon, but I just don't think I can go," I said, contributing to our current discussion on upcoming trips.

"Why not?" asked Julie. "I thought academia was supposed to be easier. Can't you take the time off?"

"Oh, I probably can, but honestly, I don't want to go." I felt so down it was hard to even discuss it, and tears came to my eyes. "I just can't stand to see another wedding. It breaks my heart to stand beside Bryan and watch a happy bride walk down the aisle to her groom." I thought of my former client's words, that he could "no longer let his own two feet take him to his abuse." Attending a wedding was nothing close to what he had experienced, but similarly, I couldn't let my own two feet take me to that heartbreak. I couldn't—I wouldn't—willingly go to another wedding with Bryan.

"Oh, Kristine . . ." they said in chorus. "Maybe Bryan will wake up one of these days," said Karen. There was nothing more to say.

The situation became more tenuous when I was approached by my alma mater, the University of Texas School of Law at Austin, to consider starting a human rights clinic at the Law School. A couple of the law professors and two brave local lawyers had been representing four detainees at Guantánamo, and there were several students informally helping them with the cases. The dean of the law school recognized a great opportunity for the law school to further develop its international law and national security programs by establishing a formal clinic, giving students the chance to actually represent Guantánamo detainees. And they wanted *me* to run the clinic.

I felt a whole host of emotions at being offered the chance to start my own law clinic—shock, fear, amazement, excitement, and doubt, to name a few—but most of all, I could hardly believe that I was being asked by UT Law to create and be the director of a law clinic (at a top-twenty school, no less), after just one year as a full-time professor. Most of the clinic directors I'd met had years of experience. It was the kind of opportunity that only comes your way once in a lifetime, and I knew it. But I also knew that moving back to Austin probably meant leaving Bryan behind, and I wasn't quite sure how I felt about that. Sure, our relationship was going through a rough spot, but it wasn't something I didn't think we could overcome together. I was willing to stay in D.C. for another year or two at AU (and then, be on the prowl for a tenure-track clinical teaching gig in D.C., which I knew would be nearly impossible to find), if Bryan could convince me that he was ready to take our relationship to the next level. Otherwise, why would I sacrifice such an incredible opportunity at UT Law?

"I just need to know if we're on the same page, here," I said. I'd told Bryan about the position I'd been offered at UT, and I knew it had come as a surprise. "This is such a great opportunity for me, but I would turn it down if I knew that we were both committed to a future together . . . like marriage."

Bryan stared straight ahead. He looked uncomfortable. If there's one thing Bryan tries to steer clear of on a daily basis, it's talking about personal issues. I pressed on.

"It's not like I'm asking you to propose *right now*," I said, thinking that's exactly what he should be doing. "It's just that, well, I can't justify passing on such an amazing opportunity for what you're offering me in exchange—a whole lot of uncertainty. If I stay at AU, I'll have to look for a job in another year or two anyway, because I have a fellowship, not a permanent position. And getting a law teaching job in this area is going to be really tough. I might have to go teach at the University of Kansas or something." I was rambling. Bryan, unlike me, does not say the first thing that comes to mind. He is a listener, an observer, a thinker, who takes his time to respond. I love those qualities about him—he is steady and calm when I am overwrought and stressed. He can soothe me with just a word or a quip.

"I *am* committed to our relationship," Bryan said. It was true; Bryan is loyal and he was committed, but I wasn't soothed.

"I mean marriage. It's time to move forward." I was trying hard to be patient.

"Why is it time? Some people take nine years to get married," Bryan responded, referring to his brother and sister-in-law, both of whom I adore. *Great. No fair comparing us to a relationship that I admire.*

"And some people get married in just a couple of years, like your brother Paul and Nancy, Paul and Andrea, Greg and Natalia," I said, naming his close friends.

"But we're not them. We're us," he said thoughtfully. Bryan didn't care what the rest of the world thought about what he did or said; he never compared himself to the Joneses or tried to be like anyone but himself. It was another quality I loved about him, but damn, at that moment I *wanted* to be the Joneses—only with three kids and a white picket fence!

"Well, one of us is moving to Austin," I said, ending the conversation.

Bryan was truly supportive of my career, and he had always been very proud of my accomplishments—even my work on the Guantánamo case, despite his general support of the Bush administration. (He's conservative, after all.) I even heard him try to explain the idea of "due process" and the importance of trials to his parents one time when he thought I wasn't listening. Then, he encouraged me to go for the UT job, suggesting that Austin was a place he would consider living.

In the end, I decided to go for it—I knew I loved Austin, I knew UT Law was a school with a great reputation, and I knew that a chance like this wouldn't come along very often (if ever). The idea of having my own clinic, being able to work on the cases that I wanted to work on, being able to call the shots—it was exhilarating after eight years of working at Shearman (where I most certainly did not call any of the shots), and then as a newbie in the law clinic at AU (where I did a lot more learning than decision making). And I knew I couldn't wait for Bryan to come through and make things right for me to stay in D.C. Maybe it was too much pressure. Maybe I wasn't the right woman for him. Maybe he was just scared. Or maybe, it didn't even matter. The point was that he wasn't ready to propose, and I couldn't wait around forever.

The next few months were spent working as usual at WCL, waiting for the formal offer to come in from UT. In the meantime, however, I felt an obligation to tell Rick that there was a very good possibility I wouldn't be renewing my fellowship for a second year. I couldn't just spring it on him—he'd been so generous in reaching out to me in the first place, and my clinic fellowship at WCL definitely had a lot to do with UT's decision to offer me a job. Plus, I knew that once Rick found out I would be leaving, he'd be on the hunt for my replacement, and I wanted to give him as much time as possible to find someone. He was disappointed, but I know he was also really proud.

Probably the only regret I have about leaving AU to open the clinic at UT was that I didn't have enough time off to take another trip like I had the year before—no second run-ins with Peruvian cows for me! I left AU in mid-July, and immediately moved to Austin to start at UT in time for the fall semester a month later. I was very lucky that my friends from law school, Megan and Brandon, still lived in Austin. They offered me their garage apartment, so I didn't have to worry about trying to find housing. It was quite nice to have an immediate family and support system in place, as I was leaving behind Bryan, my friends, and the area I'd called home for almost ten years.

I knew that my first semester in particular was going to be hard work, but I honestly didn't have any idea exactly how *much* hard work would be involved. Starting a clinic is like starting a law firm; the purpose of a law clinic is to give law students a chance to work on real cases. Every logistical aspect of running a case that a law firm must address, must also be addressed by a law clinic. It was overwhelming to be in charge of every decision, every detail, from figuring out how our students were going to call their client in Pakistan or send packages via FedEx, to troubleshooting how the students were going to file documents with the court on behalf of their client. I was in charge of it all. On top of all the logistical and administrative decisions to be made and executed, I also had to prepare to teach the class component of the clinic—a two- to three-hour lecture, once a week, along with drumming up the cases and projects for students to work on.

Thankfully, I had an extremely competent administrative assistant, Eddie, and also a recent UT Law graduate, Elizabeth Hardy, who had been working with the two UT professors and local lawyers who were representing detainees at Guantánamo. Elizabeth had already accepted a position as a clerk in the Constitutional Court in South Africa to begin in January 2008, so for both of us, it was the perfect setup: Elizabeth could gain some practical experience before starting her clerkship, and I had help getting the clinic up and running. I never could've done it without her. She helped me start the clinic from scratch and had more enthusiasm than I'd had as a recent law school graduate.

I accepted twenty students for our first semester, which I would soon learn was a lot of students for a clinic, particularly a brand-new one (ah, hindsight). Talk about a challenge! Managing a program with twenty students, where everything is new, and every question is being asked for the first time—it was a whirlwind. Despite working long nights and weekends, I kept a promise I had made to myself when I went into teaching: I was not going to give up my training and doing triathlons. I managed to do two Olympic-distance triathlons during the fall semester, placing third in my age group in one race.

I guess I thrive on stress (as Bryan always tells me), so I loved the challenge of it all—the intensity with which Elizabeth and I worked together, and the excitement shown by the students, Derek and Scott (the two UT professors), and Jack and Bill (the local lawyers whose friends thought they were crazy for representing detainees). It did occur to me yet again that I always seemed to be surrounded by men. *Why aren't there more women doing this work?*

The law school was so supportive and excited about what we were doing that at one point, when the clinic opened, the school sent out a round of press releases touting me as an authority in detainee law. That was a big moment for me, and I immediately started crafting one of my "dear Mom letters:" *Dear Mom: Guess who is a 'preeminent detainee law expert'? Can you believe it?* It was a surreal experience—to be considered "preeminent" in my field; to have landed at a firm like Shearman that handled such amazing cases in the first place; and now, to be at the University of Texas as a professor and the director of my own law clinic. It was almost too much to take in. It didn't seem possible that I had managed to accomplish so much in such a short time. I had never really had the time to reflect on my career, and it felt great. But it also felt . . . strange. I certainly hadn't considered myself an expert in my field until someone else had pointed it out.

Derek Jinks and I had been discussing changing the name of the clinic. For the fall semester, it was titled "The Rule of Law in Wartime" Clinic, because that's really what we felt was the clinic's mission, but that was a mouthful. Derek suggested putting "national security" in the title.

"Well, I think that sounds good, Derek, but 'national security'? I don't really do that stuff. I'd feel like a poseur if we called the clinic 'national security,' " I said.

"Kristine, do you realize that all of the national security textbooks and law classes in the country are teaching the cases that you have actually *worked* on?" Derek said sincerely. Derek was a nice guy, but he was not the type to feed me a line if he didn't think it wasn't true. "You're not a poseur. Do you think I suggested your name to Larry because I thought you were a poseur?" (Larry was the dean of UT Law.)

I pondered this for a moment. It had never occurred to me that I had been working on a case that might be studied in a law class. "You make a good point, Derek," I said, laughing at myself for pointing out that a law professor could make a decent argument. "But it's not like it was all me; I wasn't the lone ranger of Guantánamo detainee litigation."

"No one is saying you were, but you were certainly one of very few lawyers on the ground when this all began," Derek replied. "You've been out there, litigating these issues longer than most. You *are* an expert." The conversation struck me for one big, glaring reason: He was right. I had continued to discredit myself and my expertise because I hadn't felt comfortable considering myself an expert. Why? I had no idea; but I do know several other women lawyers and other female professionals (certainly not Jobie, but she was one of a kind) who have a hard time accepting that they are really good, maybe even an expert, at what they do. Many successful women I know talk about their success as if they had come across it by a stroke of good fortune. I always felt that way; that I was so lucky to be where I was, to have the job I did, to own my condo, etc. My mother used to say, "Kristine, that wasn't luck. You have worked really hard." I have to remind myself to believe her.

I didn't have much time to reflect, though, because in the midst of teaching, getting the clinic off the ground, and getting settled into my new life in Austin with my new family (and Judge Smith, who I had clerked for after graduating from law school ten years ago. We had stayed in touch, seeing each other every few years in Austin or D.C., with Judge Bea Ann Smith continuing to mentor me in all aspects of law and life.) helping me out, I was planning a field trip with the clinic students to D.C. The Supreme Court had finally accepted the writ of certiorari and decided to hear the *Boumediene* case (the same case my original Kuwaiti clients had been consolidated into a couple years before). It had lost big time before the D.C. Circuit Court, which had dismissed the case in early 2007. The issue—whether the Guantánamo detainees had a right under the Suspension Clause in the Constitution to challenge their detentions—was finally going to be decided. The Supreme Court was going to hear oral arguments on December 5, 2007, and I wanted my clinic students to be there. Four of the clinic students had actually worked on the briefs submitted to the Court with none other than Tom Wilner from Shearman & Sterling. Of course, it was a moment of special pride for me that my mentor, the lawyer who had helped me to become a true lawyer, was working with *my* students.

The *Boumediene* case was fairly well known, as far as court cases go, and had gotten a lot of coverage in the media. It was going to be a very popular argument to watch, and we knew we were going to have to get there early to wait in line for seats in the courtroom. We arrived in D.C. the day before the oral arguments were scheduled to begin, and my twelve students (not everyone could make the trip) got in line at six o'clock in the evening, the night before. They camped out on the steps of the United States Supreme Court (literally—although the U.S. Marshal wouldn't let them actually erect their tents), to have the chance to hear the oral argument that was going to determine the fates of their clients at Guantánamo.

I waited in a different line, since I'm a member of the Supreme Court Bar. Luckily, I didn't have to get in line until about four in the morning (instead of spending the entire night there); when it started snowing two hours later, I knew my students were going to have stories to tell when we got back to sunny Texas.

The oral arguments this time around were about whether the detainees at Guantánamo had a constitutional right to habeas corpus. Congress had passed laws—the Detainee

Treatment Act and then the Military Commissions Act—taking away their statutory rights, but the issue at hand was whether they still had rights under the Constitution, which no legislation could take away.

Even after waiting so long just to get in court, I could tell my students were thrilled to be at a Supreme Court argument for a case that some of them had worked so hard on. The highlight of the day came when the justices mentioned a case from the eighteenth century that four of my students had done a lot of research on, and written a portion of a brief about: *Three Spanish Sailors*. It's not often that research and a piece of a memo contributed by a group of law students is mentioned at the United States Supreme Court. It was their moment of glory! In anticipation of the oral argument, I had encouraged the four students to collaborate on an op-ed, to drive home my point that there's more to being an attorney than just going to court—you have to be an advocate for your clients. I was thrilled when the daily paper in Dallas, the *Dallas Morning News*, published their op-ed two days before the arguments. Talk about a great first semester!

I was much wiser when planning for the spring semester. I knew that I wouldn't have Elizabeth anymore, since she'd be in South Africa, so I accepted fewer students in the clinic. The fall semester had been hard for a variety of reasons, not the least of which was my relationship with Bryan. Although we'd decided to keep dating, we continued to struggle. When he came to visit me during that first semester, I decided enough was enough: If he didn't propose to me while he was there, I had to cut it off. I was already overwhelmed with a move to Austin, starting up a new law clinic, and getting adjusted to my new life—and I'd been spending far too much time worrying about the state of my relationship.

I was heartbroken when it came time for Bryan to leave after that visit (with no proposal), so I broke it off. It was just too difficult having my feet in two different worlds. I felt like I couldn't get settled in Austin because I'd left my heart in D.C. with Bryan. It could have been a very dark time for me, but I threw myself into my work, spent a lot of time with Megan, Brandon, and their two young boys, who call me Aunt 'Steene (short for Kristine), and trained hard, swimming, running, and biking five to six days a week.

I ended up seeing Bryan when I went back to D.C. for Thanksgiving, and to attend a friend's wedding. When he asked if I'd be coming back to D.C. for Christmas, I said, "I don't have a reason to come back." My response revealed all of the hurt I'd been holding in for the past several months. I knew it was strong language, but it was true. Austin was my home; at least, I was trying hard to make it my home. Bryan was the only thing I would've had to return to in D.C., and, in my mind, I didn't even have him anymore.

But that Thanksgiving weekend, something was different. We still obviously cared about each other, and still had a lot of fun together. Bryan had come to Uzma's wedding with me, but he seemed uncharacteristically anxious about something all weekend. Bryan was never nervous. He'd also never been one for too much introspection or chat, but I could sense something was up. We'd had a good time catching up while I was in D.C. and I'd been happy just to be next to him, but the night before I left to return to Texas, my whole life changed.

"So," he began, "do you . . . do you want to get married?"

I looked at him. I could tell that he was not asking me an academic question.

"Was that a proposal?" I asked. I couldn't believe what I was hearing. I was too shocked to even react—and too afraid to give him an answer before I'd confirmed that he had really just proposed.

Bryan nodded. "Yes," he said.

"Well, if that was a proposal, then, yes, I want to get married!"

The next morning, Bryan took me to the airport. Apparently I was still in shock from the events of the night before. *How are we going to make this work? Am I really engaged?* I hadn't dared to bring up the proposal until we'd driven up to the departures curb.

"Do you remember what you said last night?" The words came out with a squeak.

"Of course," Bryan replied, putting his arms around me.

"Ask me again," I said.

"Do you want to get married?"

I could've flown back to Austin powered by my happiness.

Suddenly, the 2007 holiday season had a whole new meaning. My parents came all the way from Alaska to the East Coast to meet Bryan's parents (who spend the winter in Vero Beach, Florida) before heading to Alabama to spend Christmas with my grandmother, and Kim and Gary, her husband of ten years, who were coming down from New York. It was a nice gathering of soon-to-be family, but I was disappointed that our engagement hadn't been made official before my parents left for Alabama. Bryan didn't make an announcement about our engagement, or even really acknowledge it. My finger was still bare, and I was starting to wonder if I'd just imagined the whole thing.

But then, the night before we left to rejoin my family in Alabama, we exchanged presents with Bryan's family. We all sat around the dining room table, with each person's presents in front of them on the table. Bryan's father opened his present first, but I have absolutely no memory of what he received, because I was too busy making eyes at the box before me. It looked suspiciously like a ring box. I eyed it, and then looked away, wondering if I could feign delight if it turned out to be a pair of earrings or a necklace, and not the engagement ring I was hoping for. (I also briefly wondered what the prison time was for murder in Florida.) When it was my turn to open my present, I unwrapped the box, opened it, and then pushed it away. I almost couldn't bear to look! Of course, curiosity got the better of me, and I opened the box to see a beautiful diamond ring. I was just staring at it, and Bryan asked impishly, "Aren't you going to put it on?" I held it out for him to slip on my finger; he was smiling like I'd never seen him smile before.

As Bryan put the ring on my finger, we kissed, and I started to cry. And as I looked around the room, I saw that Sharon (Bryan's sister-in-law) was crying, and his mom was crying—it was such a happy moment for all of us. And for Bryan, who is such a reserved person, to have made such a grand gesture in front of his family . . . It was all, finally, real.

The next semester, spring semester, was much easier. I was teaching the same lessons I'd taught in the fall, and the number of students, and, therefore, cases I had to supervise, were smaller. Not being one to just sit around, I accepted a number of speaking engagements, the most striking of which was an invitation to participate in a debate sponsored by the Oxford Union, a debating society started at Oxford University back in the 1800s. The debate was titled, "This House Would Torture to Save Lives," addressing whether or not torture should ever be used, for example, in the name of national security. Oxford debates are famous, because at the end of the debate (which resembles the English parliament in session with the same passionate yelling that goes on), the audience members actually vote on the motion by walking through the "yes" or "no" door. It was a huge honor to be invited. I traveled to Oxford at the end of January, and didn't know until I arrived that I would be the only American—and the only woman—out of six participants. Yet again, I was reminded of how male-dominated my field can be. This has got to change!

As the spring semester was coming to a close, so was another chapter in my life. I planned to spend the summer doing a little travel (two weeks in Turkey with my mom and sister), fitting in a triathlon in Austin before the trip; the rest of the time, I'd be in D.C. with Bryan, finishing plans for our upcoming wedding in August, and working on a law review article (and this book!).

Being in D.C. turned out to be a good thing for the clinic, as well. At the end of the fall semester, the Afghan clients our clinic was representing were released into Afghan custody, and in the spring semester we began representing another Guantánamo detainee—a Syrian citizen named Moammar Dokhan. Just before the semester ended, my students had drafted a habeas petition that I had planned to file in the D.C. District Court as soon as I got back to Washington. It may come as a surprise, but that habeas petition was the first document that I'd ever personally, physically filed, by myself, in court. In the past, at Shearman, I'd always had legal assistants to file for me! So there I was, the director of a legal clinic in a reputable law school, who had been an attorney for nine years, and I had managed to have several things wrong with my filing. The clerk had to help me; she showed me my mistakes, which I corrected, and pointed me in the direction of the nearest Kinko's, to scan the petition onto a CD to submit to the court, which was a rule I had apparently neglected to read. It was yet another lesson for me: *Don't ever forget where you came from.*

Three days after my "botched" petition filing, the Supreme Court issued its decision in the *Boumediene* case, the one that my students and I had traveled from Texas to hear that snowy day in December—a decision that marked a new chapter for all of the detainees that had been held for so long at Guantánamo, and also a new start for me. I had worked so hard on this very case from the beginning, in 2002, and there I was, more than six years later, about to get married and embarking on a new chapter in my own personal life. We were also on the home-stretch toward a new chapter for our country: The 2008 elections, which would put a new president in the White House, were just around the corner, and regardless of whether we ended up with a Republican or a Democratic president, Guantánamo's fate hung in the balance. Both McCain and Obama had promised to close Guantánamo, but who could be sure campaign promises would be kept? And what would closing Guantánamo mean for my Syrian client? Would he be charged or released, and where would he go?

13

Where the Hell Are We Going?

THE SUPREME COURT'S DECISION IN THE *BOUMEDIENE* CASE, which came out on June 12, 2008, was a major event, particularly in the eyes of a number of lawyers, academics, military folk, anyone interested in what was going on at Guantánamo, and anyone who cares about human rights, national security, and the future of America. It surely was a major event for me. The decision, which was revealed in a sixty-eight-page, single-spaced opinion, was a monster of a document, and a huge breakthrough for the men detained at Guantánamo. It was the decision we had been hoping for; the one I had been working toward since first being introduced to the case in March of 2002.

Basically, the Court's decision was twofold: First, the Court addressed the question of whether or not foreign citizens at the U.S. Guantánamo Bay detention center, who had been determined to be "enemy combatants," were entitled to habeas corpus. The Court's answer, detailed in pages and pages of explanation, and citing centuries-old cases and doctrines, stressed the historical importance of the habeas, which dates back to the Magna Carta. The "Great Writ," the Court wrote, is about the structure of our democracy in the United States of America. It is a defense against an arbitrary "executive," whether that executive is a king, a prime minister, or a president. Habeas, therefore, is not simply an individual's right to challenge his or her detention; it also protects our system of government, reinforces the checks and balances, and maintains the separation of the three branches of government. It is the heart of the very system our founding fathers created when they established this country.

Next, the Court went on to describe how the Guantánamo Naval Base, including the detention center, is physically controlled by the United States, and only the United States. In essence, the Guantánamo detainees have no "sovereign" power to appeal to, other than the United States. Therefore, the United States must be accountable for its actions at Guantánamo in U.S. courts. Accordingly, the Supreme Court concluded that the detainees do, indeed, have a right protected by the Constitution, to habeas, to challenge their detentions in federal court, and that right could not be "suspended" on account of the "Suspension Clause" in the Constitution, which says that habeas may not be suspended unless in time of rebellion or invasion.

I was not surprised the Court had found that the Suspension Clause of the Constitution applies to the Guantánamo detainees. The Court had decided to hear the case, meaning it was likely it would reverse the previous court's decision, which had held that the Constitution did *not* apply to the Guantánamo detainees. And it did indeed reverse the earlier decision.

It was the next part of the Court's decision that concerned my fellow habeas counsel and me. Under prevailing Supreme

Court cases, Congress can actually take away a person's constitutional right to habeas, despite the Suspension Clause, as long as the person is given an "adequate and effective" substitute. The question for the Court, then, was whether the detainees had been provided an adequate and effective substitute. The government had asserted that the CSRTs and subsequent review by the D.C. Circuit Court under the DTA were an adequate and effective substitute, but the Supreme Court found otherwise. *What a relief!* I thought. *The Court has finally come to its senses.*

The Supreme Court first examined the CSRT procedures, in which the detainees had received hearings in front of military tribunals, and then it examined the DTA review, in which the detainees were allowed to petition the D.C. Circuit for a very limited review of the original CSRT determination of "enemy combatant" status. The Supreme Court found many features of the CSRTs and the DTA review problematic; not surprisingly, those features were the same ones we had been touting for years as unjust, unfair, and inadequate. The Court didn't exactly refer to the CSRTs as "kangaroo courts," (sorry, Neil!), but it was troubled by the procedures, which did not provide a detainee any meaningful opportunity to challenge his detention. We won! We won! I had worked six long years for this day, and the feeling was indescribable. I immediately thought of my former clients (four of the Kuwaitis were still at Gitmo), and my current client. What would they think?

I was lucky to have been in D.C. when the decision came out. It was the fourth opinion by the Supreme Court in a series of opinions regarding the "war on terror," and not a single opinion had been favorable to the Bush administration. All of the legal teams who'd been waiting for this decision were immediately spurred to action; finally, after waiting for so long, it was time to get back to working on the merits of the habeas cases. Within a week of the Supreme Court's decision, the chief justice of the D.C. District Court asked counsel involved on both sides (those representing detainees and those representing the government) to come to his chambers for an informal discussion of how the cases should move forward. I was so glad to have been in D.C. for those meetings, as it meant that I'd once again be headed to court—this time as counsel for the Syrian client my UT clinic was representing.

Not all of the approximately one hundred and fifty or so lawyers who were representing Gitmo detainees worked in the D.C. area, but those of us who did, and those of us who managed to get to D.C., met in a smaller group before heading to the chief justice's chambers to discuss the upcoming meeting with the judge. Chief Justice Royce Lamberth clearly saw us as one large group, and we (the various legal teams) needed to discuss what we were going to say to the judge. It was, once again, a study in conflict resolution and diplomacy. We had a lot of different opinions, but clearly we weren't all going to be given the opportunity to speak, even though we all worked on separate cases. Each of us had a professional ethical obligation to act in the best interests of our clients—and our clients were all individual people in individual cases. Some lawyers wanted to highlight certain issues, while others wanted to tell the judge about their client's circumstances. Eventually, we agreed to disagree, deciding to explain to Judge Lamberth that we felt it wasn't necessarily fair for all of us to be forced to speak as one. Though it undermined our position, we selected a spokesperson to speak for us in the judge's chambers, a representative from CCR, and headed into the meeting.

We entered the judge's chambers, twenty-five or so lawyers representing detainees. We were the first ones there. Then the government lawyers started to file in. I had never seen so many government lawyers in one room: lawyers from the DOJ appellate division, DOJ civil division, the trial division, the court security team—probably lawyers from other government agencies I'd never worked with before, and maybe some I wasn't even supposed to know about! The judge's clerks entered, and then Judge Lamberth. We all stood up.

"I'd like to begin this informal discussion," Judge Lamberth began, "by suggesting that we go around the room and introduce ourselves individually."

It was a very nice gesture, particularly coming from a busy chief justice. Who has time for such niceties? As we introduced ourselves, I looked around at the group that had been assembled in Judge Lamberth's chambers and realized that of all the lawyers representing a Guantánamo detainee and sitting there in chambers, I was the only original lawyer there—the only attorney who had been involved since 2002. Of course, as an organization, CCR had been involved from the very beginning, but none of those original lawyers were in the room. I was it. I wished that Tom, Neil, Michael Ratner, and Joe Margulies could have been with me that day, discussing with the judge how the detainees were finally going to get their day in court, after six long years of filing after filing, oral arguments, the passage of two legislative acts intended to strip habeas from the detainees, and two trips to the Supreme Court. We had made it happen, together.

When it was my turn to introduce myself, I was sure to mention that I was teaching at UT Law. I knew that Judge Lamberth had graduated from UT Law, and that he always has a clerk from UT. A part of me was sad that I wasn't still as heavily involved as I'd been at Shearman—teaching had become a bigger priority than litigation in the years since I'd left the firm—but I was still there, and I was still just as passionate about the work I was doing. It was pretty incredible to be a part of this conversation, after so many years of hard work.

"The Supreme Court has spoken," Judge Lamberth continued. "I know the judges have stayed a lot of cases, but I've had meetings with them, and now we are ready to act. These hearings are going to go forward."

The room was completely silent. We were all somewhat dazed to be having this conversation, particularly the government lawyers.

"However," he said, "there are over two hundred habeas petitions filed, and there needs to be some coordination of these cases."

As we had discussed during our meeting, Shane Kadidal from CCR spoke for us. He explained that while we could understand why coordination might be necessary, we were all representing individual people: Some had medical issues; some had been accused of being Taliban soldiers; others were accused of being members of al-Qaeda; and some had been cleared for release but were still being held at Guantánamo. The list went on and on. Basically, Shane explained, the detainees could not be treated in court as if they were one group of exactly similar people. I felt my heart sinking; it felt like we were, in many ways, back at square one. Here we were again, trying to explain that the detainees were *people*, individuals who had been sitting at Guantánamo for years with no hearings, and that each deserved a chance—a "meaningful opportunity"—to challenge his detention. The court hearing the cases as one big group— well, that would relegate them to being faceless, nameless "detainees."

The meeting went on for at least another hour, with the government lawyers offering their thoughts on how the cases should proceed. Logistically, the government wanted complete consolidation, because it would be an easier workload from the standpoint of DOJ lawyers. Plus, treating the detainees as a faceless group of suspected terrorists would make it easier for the judge to make rulings that are less concerned with actual lives. The government lawyers also claimed that although they were going to ramp up the number of attorneys dedicated to the Guantánamo litigation, they still needed more time to develop their cases.

I could feel a sense of frustration settle over the other attorneys. *The government needed more time? Really?* It wasn't as if the government hadn't known that the Supreme Court was eventually going to make a decision on the *Boumediene* case, and they had to have realized that there was a good chance it wouldn't be decided in the government's favor. More important, the government had been holding these individuals for over six years. If the government needed more time to develop a case for holding them, then what grounds existed for holding them in the first place? Didn't the government already have plenty of reasons to be holding them? If not, then why were they being held? Despite the growing ire visible in the faces of the detainees' counsel, overall, the conversation was a very professional, congenial one. Nothing had been officially decided, however; even though Judge Lamberth had wanted to hear everyone's opinions, it was clear he was leaning toward consolidation of some sort.

Over the next couple of weeks, the lawyers for the detainees had several conversations and meetings to discuss how to address our concerns about consolidating. Consolidation, in addition to being generally unfair to the individual detainee, presented a host of other problems, including delay. Truthfully, I was in favor of some aspects of consolidation, and I was sure to say so. I'm not one to shy away from speaking my mind, even if I know it will not be well received.

We spent hours debating whether or not to fight the inevitability of consolidation, how to go about it, what items could be consolidated without putting our clients at risk, and a whole host of other issues related to consolidation. At a basic level, we each had a client involved in this, and we were each tasked with doing everything in our respective power to represent our clients most effectively. It wasn't like we could just give in and say to Judge Lamberth, "Sure, Judge, do whatever you want to do." Ultimately, however, the judge was the decision maker, and it was in our best interests to make an attempt at working together.

After two in-chambers meetings, numerous letters to the judge, an open and public hearing in court that lasted three hours, and additional briefings to the judge by both sides, Judge Lamberth decided that some sort of consolidation was necessary and would be more efficient. He assigned Judge Thomas Hogan to oversee the issues of consolidation. It all happened quickly (a good thing), but I felt that I had failed to make a contribution to our side—with one exception.

After the public hearing, Judge Hogan invited all the lawyers to submit a letter or brief to the court on any issues they wanted the court to consider. There was one in particular that was important to me: the issue of transfer. The U.S. had demonstrated that it had no trouble secreting people away to places where they were tortured by local authorities (often with the knowledge and encouragement of the U.S.). Similarly, the U.S. didn't seem to have any trouble transferring Gitmo detainees here and there. I was concerned about the possibility of illegal rendition, in which an individual is transferred to a place where it is likely he or she will be tortured. The U.S. had received a lot of criticism from the international community for its "war on terror" conduct that involved transferring people from one place to another without really making sure that they would not be tortured when they arrived at their destination. Doing so was a violation of an international treaty against torture: Basically, you can't torture, and you also can't send someone to a place where they'll be tortured.

My client, Mr. Dokhan, is a Syrian citizen, and I wanted to make sure that he couldn't be transferred out of Guantánamo to Syria without my knowledge and without his permission, because I wanted to have the ability to try to stop his transfer if I felt that it would put him in danger. The government, of course, was opposed to even providing notice of the possible transfer of a detainee out of Guantánamo, to his home country or anywhere else. The issue of transfer had fallen by the wayside during the public hearing, but for me, it was one of the most important issues. I submitted a letter on behalf of my client with my request for thirty days' notice, and a week later, Judge Hogan issued an order granting not only my request, but also requiring the government to supply thirty days' notice to *all* detainees' counsel before a transfer was made. I was victorious! I had spent years and years filing motions, requests, and letters, asking for some of the most simple items and conditions for the detainees, and the court had rarely even bothered to rule on most of the requests we had filed. I had finally prodded the court to action!

My success was the highlight of that summer—at least from a work standpoint. Litigation is time-consuming and cumbersome, a debate on paper that never ends. We spent the majority of the second half of 2008 filing briefs, and the government stalled and delayed at every point, claiming more time was needed. Though the government was required by court order to begin submitting its reasons for holding the detainees (called a "factual return") in late August 2008, there were once again requests for more time, which the court allowed, citing national security concerns. Truthfully, the court *should* be concerned with national security—terrorism against the U.S. is a reality—but how much longer can the people at Guantánamo hold on before they are finally allowed to have their day in court? Should the government's bureaucracy and ineptitude keep innocent people in prison, or keep it from charging those detainees who are suspected of committing terrorism?

Unfortunately, it wasn't just the government that seemed to have difficulty moving forward. Judge Hogan, though well-intentioned, took almost three months to issue an order setting out the procedures for hearing the habeas cases. The most alarming part of the order was that he gave the attorneys for the detainees a brief fourteen to twenty-eight days from the time they received the government's "factual return" to submit a response (called a "traverse") as to why the detainee shouldn't be detained. The government had had *six years* to put its cases together; we would have less than a month. And, in many cases, the attorneys, me included, had no real information as to why the government was holding our clients, and wouldn't until the government filed its factual returns. That started the clock ticking—twenty-eight days to try to figure out how to disprove the government's allegations, find witnesses (who were all overseas), visit Guantánamo (which requires twenty-one days' notice prior to visits) to meet with the client, write a brief, and do discovery. It was effectively removing our clients' rights to habeas all over again, albeit in a different way. How could there be a meaningful opportunity to challenge the detention under those circumstances?

Fortunately, 2008 wasn't merely a series of frustrations. During the spring semester, well before the *Boumediene* decision was issued, two of the UT clinic's clients (Afghan citizens) who had been detained, first at Guantánamo and then at Policharki Prison in Bagram, Afghanistan, were released to freedom after never being charged. My UT students had worked diligently throughout the year on behalf of these men, filing a flurry of petitions and motions, in order to achieve a result that, at the time, had seemed all but impossible.

One of these students, Carter Thompson, also spent a number of frustrating hours trying to track down other Afghan clients who had been released in 2007, hiring a private investigator, finding a translator, and finally making contact with one of the men who had made it back to his village in Afghanistan, near the border of Pakistan. Carter later relayed to me the emotion he felt when he spoke on the phone with the former client, an unknown individual he had been trying to help for months. "That I was talking with a real live person was overwhelming," Carter said to me in my office. "But when he thanked me over and over for our help, it hit me like a ton a bricks: I felt like I had really done something. All that lawyering finally meant something."

The past year had been a rewarding time for me personally, as well. I completed four triathlons, and placed in my age group in two of them. And then there was the most important event: Bryan and I were married in Alaska on August 15 in front of seventy of our family and friends. It was amazing, and wonderful, and a really great way to solidify the foundation for the next chapter in my life—focusing on family, and Bryan, and putting myself first for a while, instead of living my work, day in and day out.

I had realized, a while back, that I'd sacrificed a lot for my work; I'd been working so hard that I hadn't even noticed it. In the end, I have a whole new appreciation for how much more important my life—which is not all work—is to me now. I'd spent so much time fighting for the ability of my clients to have the right to continue living their lives, should they be found innocent; but I hadn't done the same for myself.

This change in my work, and my outlook on life, isn't the only change ahead for my future. The year 2008 has ushered in a new era in American politics. The Bush administration, under which Guantánamo came into being, will be making an exit, and a new administration will be in charge. At the beginning of the summer, I was asked if I would like to be nominated to serve on an advisory committee to Barack Obama. Despite all of my upcoming commitments, I said yes. I couldn't help myself. I was excited about being part of his campaign, and maybe even being able to contribute something based on my Guantánamo and national security expertise.

To my disappointment, however, I was nominated to be on the Immigration Advisory Committee, which addressed traditional domestic border and immigration issues, of which I know very little, and my AU immigration experience wasn't going to cut it. Then the *Boumediene* decision came out and I became a litigator again overnight, going to court and filing briefs. And then, of course, there was the wedding to plan. As much as I wanted to, I couldn't keep up with the activities of Senator Obama's committee, though I continued to watch from the sidelines. If I'm lucky, maybe there will be a time and place for me to rejoin the fight and really try to contribute something of significance.

When I returned to Guantánamo in October and December 2008 to visit my last remaining client, I was disheartened to be reminded of just how depressing a place it is. Little has changed there for the detainees and our servicemen and -women who guard them, but with a new, history-making administration on its way in, I am hopeful that 2009 and the years that follow will bring change for all.

AFTERWORD

It had been an emotional week for me. After my month-long academic winter break, I left Bryan behind in Arlington to return to Austin in order to begin the 2009 spring semester, where I would be teaching and running the National Security Clinic at UT Law School. It would be my last semester, as I would return permanently to the Washington, D.C., area to live with my husband and try to start a family.

On Monday, January 19, 2009—Martin Luther King Day—the day after I returned to Austin, my niece and goddaughter was born. Lily Pauline Maurer, or "Lulu," as she was called by her parents while in the womb, had arrived six days early. I think she was excited to come into the world, just as excited as those who braved the cold and crowds in D.C. or the millions who tuned in to see history in the making. Lulu had to witness for herself the inauguration of President Barack Obama, the first black U.S. president, who also happens to be of mixed race and ethnicity, just like her. Obama's inaugural address spoke of challenges, of core values, and of change. And when I listened to the words and thought of my new niece (Kim and Gary's first child, and my parents' first grandchild), I couldn't help but think of the new beginnings for the Huskey family, for me, for all of America, and for the men detained at Guantánamo.

On January 22, the first day of class for the National Security Clinic, President Obama issued several executive orders, one of which called for the closing of the Guantánamo Bay Detention Center within one year. I couldn't believe it. He had run his campaign on that promise, among others, but I did not expect that by the second day in office, President Obama would issue such an order. Seven years and eleven days after the first detainee had been brought to the Guantánamo prison, the president had issued an order for its closure. There would be no "Guantánamo," a name that evoked a variety of images in both proponents and opponents of the detention center: blindfolded and shackled men in orange jumpsuits, hardened terrorists, hunger strikers, jihadists, indefinite detention, torture.

My new students wondered whether we'd have any work to do. "Guantánamo is shutting down—what will we do?" they asked me. In addition to the fact that my clinic handles a number of cases and projects relating to national security other than Guantánamo, I knew that shutting Guantánamo would be neither easy nor the end of the story. Closing Guantánamo would not erase what the last administration had done to vastly undermine America's global reputation as a champion of human rights; nor would it undo the torture and abuse that many men at Gitmo had suffered. We would have to work hard as a nation to earn back our reputation, and those now in power would have to think carefully about whether some individuals in the Bush administration should be prosecuted for war crimes. I knew we could achieve the first, but I was not so sure we would pursue the latter.

Closing Guantánamo meant that something had to be done

with the individuals there. We could release them back to their countries of origin, unless they were likely to be tortured. In that case, international law dictates that we send such individuals to a "safe" third country. But who would accept these men who had been labeled as "enemy combatants," in many cases wrongly? Another option would be to prosecute them under federal criminal laws in our federal courts for crimes such as terrorism, conspiracy to commit terrorism, or even "material support for terrorism." Trials in the United States for terrorism-related activity had been taking place since the laws existed; after 9/11 the number simply increased, and several "terrorists" became well-known, such as John Walker Lindh (the "American Taliban") and Moussaoui (the "twentieth hijacker"). But some proponents of Guantánamo had expressed concern over this option, claiming that the evidence wouldn't stand up in court, that there wasn't enough evidence, that there was too much classified (secret) evidence—all obstacles to a conviction, which some regarded as the end goal, rather than the consequence of a fair process.

There was a third option: In addition to the first two courses of action, we could continue to detain "suspected terrorists." In other words, we could detain people who had not actually committed any crime, but whom we thought *might* commit some terrorist act or harm the national security of America. These would be people we considered "too dangerous" to release or even transfer to the custody of another country and who we could not charge and try in court due to lack of evidence or other related problems. This third option is evident in Obama's executive orders. While requiring the closure of Guantánamo, it also calls for the creation of a "Special Interagency Task Force on Detainee Disposition" and allows for the possibility that individuals "apprehended in counterterrorism operations," not just those currently at Guantánamo, could be detained "in the interest of national security." This course of action—preventive detention—was, in fact, what we were doing under the Bush administration! Would Obama continue such a policy, just more humanely and in accordance with domestic and international laws?

I remembered the lines from the president's inaugural address that had struck home for me: "As for our common defense, we reject as false the choice between our safety and our ideals. Our founding fathers, faced with perils we can scarcely imagine, drafted a charter to assure the rule of law and the rights of man, a charter expanded by the blood of generations. Those ideals still light the world, and we will not give them up for expedience's sake."

The rule of law and the rights of man *are* ideals that light the world; they are America's ideals, and they always have been no matter how hard the last administration tried to act otherwise. But terrorism is a reality that we can't simply ignore. No one wants another 9/11. Can we forge a new policy that protects both our national security and our founding fathers' ideals? The year 2009 will indeed bring much change and many challenges, and I believe in going forth to meet them that we *will* remain true to our values, that we will not falter in our virtue. I have hope.

INDEX

Index

U.S. Government
    access to detainee information,
        142–45, 153–58
    Boumediene delay, 264–66
    denial of basic rights, 157, 199–202
    detainee treatment, 189–90
    detention policy, xiii–xiv, 149–50
    fear mongering, 160–61
    loss of faith in, 217
    national security arguments,
        198–200, 255, 268
    "Saying It Doesn't Make It So"
        argument, 165–66
    support of UNITA in Angola, 6

U.S. Supreme Court
    Boumediene v. Bush, 249–51,
        256–57
    Boumediene decision, 258–61
    clerking for Justice Stevens, 108
    decision on challenging
        detention, xi
    Rasul v. Bush appeal, 167–72
    Rasul v. Bush decision, 172–75,
        178–80, 195–96

UT. *See* University of Texas (UT) Law
    School

Vietnam conflict, 134

Volunteer Lawyers for the Arts, 87

war crimes, 225, 232–36

"war on terror," 156, 166, 168–69,
    260–61, 266–67

Washington, D.C.
    arrival as second year associate,
        105–6
    9/11 attacks, 136–37, 172
    Shearman & Sterling office, 95–101

Washington College of Law, 221, 245

The Washington Post, 163

Weintraub (Professor), 81–82

Wet Paint (restaurant), 43

"white-shoe" law firms, 158

Wilner, Tom, viii–xi, 116–21, 171, 250,
    262–63

Wilson, Rick, 221–23, 232–33, 237–38,
    245

Windward Side (Gitmo), viii, 184, 233

women
    detainee abuse by, 207–9
    in detainee law, 237, 247–48
    in Kuwaiti culture, 145–47, 150–53
    in a male-dominated field, 255
    as "one of the boys," 120–21
    as role models, 93, 113
    seeing self as expert, 248–49

Woody's (music club), 42

The World (NYC dance club), 29

World Medical Association (WMA),
    210, 213

Xenakis, Stephen, 213–14

Yahoo!, 232

Yugoslavia, 1–2, 10

Zaire, 1

ABOUT THE AUTHORS

KRISTINE A. HUSKEY IS A CLINICAL PROFESSOR AND THE DIRECTOR of the National Security Clinic at the University of Texas School of Law in Austin, Texas. She is also a fellow at the Robert S. Strauss Center for International Security and Law. She spent eight years as an attorney practicing international litigation and arbitration at the law firm of Shearman & Sterling in Washington, D.C. She has also taught at a number of law schools: the International Human Rights Clinic at Washington College of Law, American University, Howard University School of Law, George Washington University School of Law, and Victoria University Law School in Wellington, New Zealand.

Professor Huskey has represented several individuals detained as "enemy combatants" at Guantánamo, including Omar Khadr, the young Canadian citizen to be charged under the Military Commissions Act, and a group of Kuwaiti citizens in the seminal *Rasul v. Bush* case, in which the U.S. Supreme Court held in 2004 that the Guantánamo detainees have a right to challenge their detentions. As the director of the National Security Clinic, she has worked and supervised students on national security and human rights cases and projects involving Guantánamo, the military commissions, Muslim charities, the right to privacy, the Patriot Act, illegal rendition, and the use of private security companies, such as Blackwater, in areas of armed conflict.

Professor Huskey has been the recipient of several awards, including the 2008 Public Interest Award by the Travis County Women Lawyers' Association; the 2007 Frederick Douglass Human Rights Award by the Southern Center for Human Rights, for her pro bono work representing detainees at Guantánamo Bay (awarded to all attorneys representing detainees); the 2007 Pro Bono Service Award by Human Rights USA, for work seeking accountability for human rights abuses in China; and the 2002 Outstanding Achievement Award by Washington Lawyers' Committee for Civil Rights and Urban Affairs, for her pro bono work in an employment discrimination case. The UT Clinic was recently awarded the Best Defenders of Habeas Corpus award in the *Austin Chronicle*'s Best of Austin 2008 awards.

Huskey was also featured as a "Woman to Watch" in *Marie Claire* magazine in December 2006 and was the subject of "Working Women" on ABC News. She has published several articles, and is a contributing author to *One of the Guys: Women as Aggressors and Torturers*.

After growing up in Alaska, Kristine lived and traveled all over the world. She competes in triathlons as often as she can, and loves to cook, drink wine, go dancing, and fish and hunt with her family in Alaska. She currently splits her time between Austin, Texas, where she teaches, and Arlington, Virginia, where she lives with her husband.

Aleigh Acerni is a writer and editor who began her career as a writer, columnist, and assistant editor for a regional newspaper in the Southeast. Since 2005, she has been an editor for *skirt!*, a monthly women's magazine with nineteen print markets across the United States. She has written about everything from gardening to women's issues, and her news articles, columns, features, and personal essays have appeared in various regional and national publications. She has interviewed celebrities such as playwright Eve Ensler, actresses Kristin Davis and Virginia Madsen, and pioneering chef Alice Waters.

Acerni has served as a panelist for the Society of Professional Journalists and the Southern Regional Press Institute, and has judged student award competitions for the Society of Professional Journalists' Mark of Excellence Awards and the Catholic Press Association's Press Awards.

Currently, Acerni lives and works in Charlotte, North Carolina, with her husband and two rescued golden retriever mixes. She loves to cook, drink champagne, and tries not to neglect her yoga mat. *Justice at Guantánamo* is her first book.